WILL

The front page of Bill's Diary.

1st Edition

Published in 2016 by

Woodfield Publishing Ltd
www.woodfieldpublishing.co.uk

ISBN 978-1-84683-176-8

Printed and bound in England

Typesetting & page design: Nic Pastorius
Cover design: Jeanette Upshall/Klaus Schaffer

Source document
Will's War by Jeanette Upshall (final)

Wills' War

A Soldier's Experiences with the Somerset Light Infantry in India & Mesopotamia 1913-19

JEANETTE UPSHALL

Woodfield

Woodfield Publishing Ltd

Bognor Regis ~ West Sussex ~ England ~ PO21 5EL

tel 01243 821234 ~ **e/m** info@woodfieldpublishing.co.uk

Interesting and informative books on a variety of subjects

For full details of all our published titles, visit our website at
www.woodfieldpublishing.co.uk

In loving memory of
Mum and Dad
Marjorie and Eric Upshall.

Dad I have kept my promise to you
but I am sad that you cannot read it.

Private William Ralph Upshall
in "Dress Uniform".

Contents

Acknowledgements

Many people in Evercreech have provided me with useful information on, for example, the name of a Lane or a Road that has since altered; and I would particularly like to thank Gill and David Lindsay for providing me with a copy of the newspaper cutting and photographs of Tom Edwin Upshall.

May I also thank my cousin Sylvia Lintern, my Aunt Valerie Foster and my cousin Philip Roper for their help and their many chats regarding the family and also providing me with numerous family photographs.

I would like to say a big thank you to Tom Upshall for his patience and racking his brain to remember his grandmother Caroline Upshall, and describing her little mannerisms and giving me an insight into her character; and also a huge thank you to his lovely wife, Dot, for providing cups of tea.

I am very grateful also to my Aunt Josie Quimby in Maine, U.S.A for her letter and photographs she sent over to me and for providing me with an email address for my cousin Maureen McHugh. With the help of my cousin Maureen and her many emails , I was able to piece together some of the missing links needed in my story.

May I also add finally my thanks to the wonderful Somerset Heritage Centre in Taunton, who enabled me to link all my grandfather's notes to actual facts concerning the Somerset Light Infantry, without whom none of this might have been possible. The enormous efforts they make of taking care of old documents is sheer delight. The enjoyment I had in putting on lycra gloves and carefully placing the old files onto small cushions was well worth the while.

Jeanette Upshall, November 2016.

A little leather wallet with inside his father's diary and photographs of WW1.

Prologue

The fact that this book is here at all is all down to circumstance and an accident when Dad fell off a chair in his bedroom whilst reaching for something on top of his wardrobe. He knocked his shoulder quite badly and went to see his doctor. This worried Mum straight away, as Dad only visited a doctor if he was at the end of his tether, in a lot of pain, or thought he was 'coming down with something awful' and then only if paracetamol hadn't done the trick.

Mum insisted on going with him, as always, and his doctor, a very nice lady, realised when examining him that something was not as it should be and made an appointment directly with the nearby hospital for an X-ray and a scan. This on its own was enough to put Dad off right there and then and it got him really in a fret.

A series of visits to the local hospital followed, eventually resulting in Dad being diagnosed with a trapped nerve in his right shoulder, explaining why he couldn't use his right hand properly. But the scans also revealed a worse diagnosis; Dad had prostate cancer.

Mum phoned me one day and I could tell straight away that something was bothering her. You know how it is when someone very dear to you calls with a certain tone in their voice and you sense that all is not as it should be? Mum wasn't as fit as she'd like to think she was and without hesitation I realised I had to be there for her.

Both my sisters had busy working lives of their own and as I only worked voluntarily off and on, so it seemed obvious to me that I should be there for Mum and Dad. I am the middle sister of three and live in Holland with my grown-up daughter. My son had already married and settled in nearby Lelystad in his own home with his lovely wife. I had no other ties, as I had been divorced for almost 10 years. After talking things over with both my children and explaining the situation, they both agreed that it was best that I go. Mum and Dad meant a lot to both of them and it was also very nice to hear them both say, "We would do the same in your position, Mum."

To be honest with you, I think my daughter was quite excited at the thought of living for an unlimited period of time in an apartment on her own, in her own space, and I can't say I blame her.

I booked a flight (no return), packed my suitcase with an assortment of clothing and off I went...

Lots of visits to the local hospital in Yeovil followed and Dad seemed to be coping with it all, like he did with most problems, and tried to keep his head up and stay focused and positive.

But we could all see a different Dad over the following months. We ladies all know that men seem to have more trouble with any illness, even a simple cold can be a problem, let alone a more serious one. Dad was a very stubborn man and felt he could still do everything, even though his right hand had now become almost unusable.

It was during my stay with them both that Dad began talking about his father. He was remembering the 'good old days' and generally reminiscing about his childhood with his parents in Evercreech and the things he got up to. You know the kind of things I'm talking about? It's what older people tend to do and it is not only interesting to hear but does everyone a lot of good too. But why, oh why, do these memories only occur when time seems to be running out?

One day Dad held out a photograph of his father for me to see.

"That's Dad in his Army uniform, when he first joined the army before the First World War broke out," he said.

The picture was no bigger than the old cigarette cards I'd also watched Dad look through and show me. When I looked at that picture I saw a very young boy standing upright and proud and all I could utter was, "Oh". I asked Dad how old would he have been and he thought probably about 16 years old. I said I thought he looked only about 12! Dad just smiled at me, turned in his reclining chair and struggled, but managed, to pick up a light brown leather wallet.

"I've got something interesting to show you now," he said.

I turned to look at Mum.

"Hmm, you'd better sit down love, or you'll get a crick in your neck leaning over like that," she said. She was knitting all the time she was looking at me and smiling her usual lovely smile. *How does she do that?* I thought to myself, *knit and not look at her work and talk to me at the same time?*

I grabbed the small footstool which Dad had bought Mum to rest her feet on but which Mum never really used. She was very stubborn at times too. I felt I needed to look up at Dad and get as close to him as possible. I could tell by the twinkle in his eye that what he was about to show me inside this wallet was a treasure he had kept very close to his heart. This was suggested by the simple fact that since not feeling well, the picture of Granddad had never left his side (he kept it on his side of the living room mantelpiece). The leather wallet was also by his side, kept on an old antique trolley, with all his vintage car club magazines, his own diary and various other books. You see Mum and Dad had their little treasures on each side of the hearth. On Mum's side she kept a square box (which acted as an extra chair when unexpected visitors came) where all her knitting patterns were kept, along with various photograph albums holding precious holiday memories and pictures of their grandchildren.

First of all Dad pulled out of the wallet a pocket notebook; it was missing its cover and back and the pages were faded and curling at the edges. The handwriting (which I could just about see) was that of an older person, I thought, and looked very neat. Dad was flipping through the pages and I could see that he was looking for something in particular. It appeared to have a lot of empty pages, I noticed, so I was wondering what it was he was looking for.

"Ah... here it is," he said with relief. "I've found the beginning!"

The beginning of what? I was wondering. He kept the pages open, turned the notebook around and handed it to me, with this big smile on his face, saying, "What d'you make of this then?"

What he had searched for in that little notebook, as I quickly scanned the page and read some of the words, sent a shiver down my spine and I felt butterflies fluttering in my stomach!

"Is this a diary your Dad kept while he was in the Army?" I asked.

"Aha, what do you reckon? Could you make something of it and write some kind of story for me?" Dad looked at me in such a way that I felt flattered by his question.

"I can try to make something of it," I said, looking around for my reading glasses. The writing was very tiny and not that clear in parts.

"He wrote that with a purple pencil," Dad said. "He used to tell me that that was what was given to him to write with so as not to fade as easily as an ordinary lead pencil."

Looking more closely at the pages, now with my glasses on, I noticed that much of what my Granddad had written down consisted of dates and places and small sentences. Here and there were notes jotted up the side of the page and there were some pages that had smudges on them, possibly from getting wet. It began with: *Enlisted 1913...* and on the last page it had *10/4/1919 Got home about eight in the morning.*

At the front of the notebook, which would have been the first page if the cover had still been there, were names and addresses of, I presumed, family members.

"How you expect Jeanette to fathom all that out and make something of it, I'm sure I don't know," said Mum, knitting away at such a speed that the needles were making up their own tune in the process. I could almost imagine smoke coming from them, such was the rate she was going at!

"Well, she can have a go at it, can't you love?" Dad looked so questioningly at me that I couldn't even hesitate and said I certainly would love to have a go at it. Meanwhile Dad was pulling out some more things from the wallet. These were photographs.

"Dad told me that he kept these with the notebook and said he'd taken them during his time over in India."

I hadn't got to the stage of making out where my Granddad had actually gone during the war, but apparently he'd gone to India.

The pictures were faded too. Well, stupid me, I guess they would be after all this time. They were mostly sepia coloured, with the exception of a few in black and white. Some had folds in them or the corner had fallen off over the years but apart from that, they seemed alright. They nearly all had a name written in pencil on the back of them, which would be very handy for me in identifying where they had been taken. I thought how precise he had been, especially when you consider this was all done in the War and probably during battle conditions.

"Well... what d'you think?" Dad said, and by the way he looked at me again, I knew that he was being very serious about all this and really wanted me to try.

"It all looks very interesting Dad and I will get straight on it," I said.

The back two pages were just handwritten lists of dates, places and sums of money with, at the very end of the column of numbers, a total amount.

"That was how much Dad got paid each time. Ha-ha, he obviously wanted to make sure he got that all noted down. He was a stickler when it came to money!"

I had never realised that soldiers in the Great War got paid for their services too, or am I just being ridiculous in not realising that?

"Now, let's have a cup a tea!" Dad said, licking his lips.

"Bout time too, my mouth is so dry I can't spit sixpence," agreed Mum, who had now put her knitting down to look at both of us, as if to say, 'enough of that'.

Dad handed over the leather wallet and I carefully slid the photographs into the right hand side and the little diary in the left. The wallet felt soft and nice to the touch and I knew then that I would treasure it forever.

❖ ❖ ❖

Somewhere over the brow of the Hill
There's an end of strain and strife
The promise and fulfilment
of the good and happy life

Somewhere over the brow of the Hill
There's a place where Sunlight gleams,
And golden fields where one can reap
The Harvest of their dreams

Private 2025 William Ralph Upshall
2/4 Somerset Light Infantry, 1913.

My Story

My name is William Ralph Upshall, but you can call me 'Bill'. Almost everyone calls me Bill and to be honest with you, I prefer it.

I've got something I feel I want to share with you. I've kept quiet for too long now and it's time to let it go. This has been a part of me that changed my life completely. Five years of my life, as a matter of fact. I changed from a very naïve Bill into an open-minded, young-manly Bill. I, who had hardly stepped out of the county of Somerset, let alone travel to another country, was about to travel to the other side of the world.

Why should I tell you my story, you might ask yourselves? Well why not? I have gone through an awful lot in my teenage years and so have my family. I have no regrets that I enlisted in the War as I feel I did the right thing at the time, but no-one could ever anticipate the time it would take to end that war. No wonder it was called the 'Great War' later on in life. However, there was nothing 'great' about it. Not to me and certainly not to the poor chaps in Europe.

I am hoping you won't come across a book quite like mine. If you have, however, encountered such a book, then please forgive me for imagining otherwise.

All of us, I am grateful to say, explain incidents that occur in other fashions and sometimes even the way a story is told can make the difference between it being rather boring or quite interesting. I would certainly never want to be a bore to anyone and through my whole life I have tried to take matters as they arise and never be too serious, unless it absolutely can't be avoided.

Family members that have known me would most likely tell you that I can be witty when I want to be and love to have a good time. I have always had pleasure in making other people laugh and have great enjoyment in dressing up.

I hope you enjoy reading *my story*.

The only problem is where to begin? Well, I would like to point out that after pondering this for a couple of days, I've decided to begin by explaining me, 'Bill', and where I come from. It's as good a place as any to start a story, wouldn't you agree? So let's get on with it then...

❖ ❖ ❖

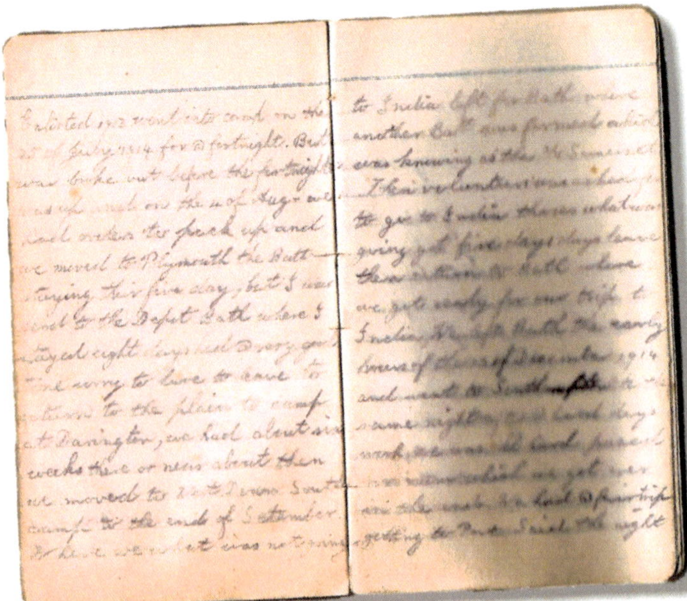

First of all he pulled out of the wallet a pocket notebook. "I've found the beginning!" The beginning of what I was wondering? He kept the pages open and turned it around and handed it to me, with this big smile on his face. "What d'you make of this then?"

1913

My Family

I come from a proud generation of Upshalls, of which, in fact, our family are from the 4th generation, or so I've been told by my dad. Mind you, that's if you take the time to delve back into the past, I reckon the amount of generations he goes back is pushing it a bit though; he is probably 'pulling my leg', as the saying goes, with that bit. My father has kept his memory of his previous grandfathers all 'up in ere', as he will often say to me, pointing to his head in such a way that always makes me laugh. But then we are, like I said, a proud generation and, well, we just seem somehow to keep in touch and tell each other stories of the past. And that's the way it should be. You should get to grips with your family and talk to them. My grandfather's name was Jeremiah but he died before I was born and I also never met my grandmother, whose name was Mary Ann. Most of our relations live in the county of Dorset, so we don't get to see them that often.

I love to sit in the evenings by the fireside and listen to Dad talk about his family. The names used to make me laugh when I was little. Such names as Theophilus would get me giggling or perhaps it was the way Dad would say it, kind of slow like *thé...o...* and quickening at the end *phi-lus*.

There was many a George mentioned too and one in particular was married to a Miss Unity Eyres, which has a certain ring to it. I used to conjure up all sorts of visions about her; thinking with a name like that she could even be a film star. She wasn't though. Then names like Tryphene, who was a daughter of Jeremiah, come to mind. Dad reckons my great-great-grandfather called one of his boys Solomon, which he took from the Bible.

Of course many names have held their popularity down through the line of Upshalls and are used many times over, as is the case in most families. Like the name George and both of Dad's names, Thomas and William, have been carried throughout and I am very pleased to be one of those Williams!

My dad is called Thomas William Upshall and was born in a place called Sturminster Newton and Mum's name is Caroline Mary. Mum came from Dorset too but from another village called Stalbridge.

Dad has always worked on a farm but came to Somerset to get a job on the Somerset and Dorset Railway Line, which he did manage to accomplish for a while. He is a hard worker and a very kind man.

Dad loved to tell us a story or too and one day, when most of us kids were at home sitting about, he got to talking about his family again and then he said, "when times get a bit rough you 'ave to do sometimes drastic things to make it better. I reckon I did the right thing though, now I look back on it. You see this ole farmhouse was thatched and it were in so bad repair that I went and set fire to it. Then I went and sold the house and land for what I could. I'll show you lot how I reaped me seeds that day." He nipped upstairs like a shot and in no time was back in the room with an old tin box. He unlocked it with a very small key and took out a wad of notes.

"Here wha's think about this lot then?" he said, and got us all around his chair to lay our eyes on his treasure. "Ere, ave a hold a that then."

We were all allowed to hold it carefully and even smell it. I don't know what it is about the smell of money, but it's got a special smell all of its own.

"You'll most likely never get to 'old that much money in your lives," he told us. It was a fortune to all of us and we were actually

My dad is called Thomas William Upshall and was born in a place called Sturminster Newton, Dorset.

Mum's name is Caroline Mary Cole and she came from Stalbridge, Dorset.

told not to talk of it to anybody outside the house. But on that particular day we sat in awe and wonder, our eyes popping out of our little heads with sheer amazement at so much wealth that our own father had in his possession. That memory will stick in my mind forever.

Dad hasn't a lot of hair nowadays but makes up for this with his moustache, which he proudly keeps tidy and I will often find him of an evening sat down in his favourite old chair combing it in front of Mum's hand mirror! It's not a huge moustache as moustaches go, but curves from one lower cheekbone over his upper lip down to the other.

He always washes after a long day of work on the farm before having his supper and changes his shirt and trousers. It's a ritual that we boys have all felt a need to copy out of simple respect for Mum and her utmost effort in keeping our cottage tidy and putting meals on the table.

Mum has her work cut out raising us, washing our clothes and all the general domestic chores a mother has to do. How she manages to keep herself always looking so neat and tidy I will never know. She has kind eyes like Dad's and is patient in nature. Her hair is always kept tied back with a kind of knot at the back of her head and if anybody were to ask me how long Mum's hair is, I would not be able to answer, as I have never seen her hair untied, believe it or not. It must be the first thing she does early in the morning and the last thing at night, because I can't imagine her sleeping like that. Well, it wouldn't be very comfortable now would it, lying on a knot? And anyway, I've watched how some of my sisters have done the same thing.

I must tell you another thing that my Mum does, which I noticed more as a little boy playing on the floor. Mum *glides* around a room with so much grace and easiness that it will often take my breath away. This could be because of her skirts and dresses that not quite touch the floor or maybe because I can never quite see her feet. Anyhow, I thought I'd just let you know, Mum never just walks but glides and it's mesmerizing.

I have grown up in Somerset in a small village called *Evercreech*. I live in a small cottage (the second one from the road) at Backway Lane. As you might think when reading the word 'backway', the lane is so called for the most obvious reason of all; it is down a back lane! The road I mention goes no further than around the corner of our row of cottages and then it stops. A 'dead-end', you might say. Although the road, or maybe I should say the lane, stops, there is a narrow pathway on further, which then also branches off into two directions. You can either carry straight on past small allotment patches and down a slight slope and come out at the side of Weymouth Road; or you can take the left-hand pathway, which actually I think of more as a darker alleyway, as it has walls on either side, and you would come out at the top end of Weymouth Road. Either way, is a pleasure to walk or ride the bicycle if you want to short-cut the road, but riding a bicycle takes a little more skill and you have to watch out for anyone walking because the alley is too narrow to pass by. When I was little I used to get scared of turning to the left of the alleyway, as it seemed to go on forever and look quite sinister of an evening. It also has its own nickname too; we call it *The Drain a*nd will more than likely say "we are off down the drain" when we take this route.

Our house is just a modest cottage, like most cottages in Evercreech. It has two bedrooms upstairs and two rooms downstairs, one for sitting in and the other being the kitchen. Outside, at the back of the cottage, we have our 'outhouse' (that's a lavatory to be precise). Of course, now the more modern houses are lucky enough to enjoy this 'inside' and not out! They won't realise how privileged that will be to them. We have also a small garden at the front, which is left pretty much for my mother to take care of and our vegetable patch at the back of the cottage being, of course, the proud ownership of my father. When I say 'ownership' I don't really mean literally but I mean figuratively speaking because

Mum does help when the need arises. The vegetable patch is my father's pride and joy. He grows just about every vegetable he possibly can, space allowing that is. He takes great pleasure in growing his vegetables too. And, if they turn out to be almost perfect in shape and colour, he will enter them in the local show, which is held here every summer. Has he won prizes with them? Yes, he most certainly has.

Getting back to the cottage, "it's cosy and comfortable and it suits us" are the very words my dad uses to describe it. I mustn't forget to mention the fireplaces in each room. Why? Well, they are the hub of any family. Anyone will tell you that. I can't imagine anything cosier than sitting around an open hearth, whatever the weather is outside. Well, not if it's really hot outside, of course. Then you wouldn't light a fire. That would just be silly and a waste of good wood, now wouldn't it? But otherwise, *yep*, it's just great.

Surrounding the village are plenty of fields and several farms too. I like to go for long walks in these fields and I enjoy walking down to see the local farmers and watch them work. Of course, I not only stand about idly and watch. No, if they'll let me then I'm only too glad to help out. I like milking the cows. I can't really explain why I like milking them, but I just seem to find it quite rewarding. Sometimes I can get a whole bucketful of milk from only the one cow. Mind you it's back aching work, that it is. If I help a farmer out with his milking, then he lets me take home a tumbler full for Mum. This she appreciates very much and the farmer will often get a bag of potatoes in return, or whatever we've got enough of at that time.

There are five local pubs in the village but I like to walk down the road to probably the farthest of the five as there is a stream which runs from the bottom of Weston Town all the way down the back of the pub and it also has a watermill. Actually, it isn't a pub but an Inn. It is aptly called Pecking Mill. On the way down the road me and Jesse would stop at the little bridge and lean over to throw in sticks, which sometimes we'd make into boats with leaves for sails, and watch them come out the other side. Now, I've fallen in this stream a couple of times; when I was younger, of course. You know how it is, you get curious when you're little and see a shiny something on the bottom, lean over to try and reach it and the next thing you are fighting for your sweet little life, gasping for air and your big brother is trying to grab hold of you or anything on you to get you out of there as quickly as possible.

Yes, this has happened to me a few times. And you know the worst thing about an incident like this isn't the falling in the water or being cold when you're pulled out. No, it's hearing your mum give your brother a good old telling-off for not watching out for you like he should have done in the first place. That is the worst part of all. Not that any harm would come to him, or me for that matter, apart from a clip around the ear and the odd chore we'd have to do to make up for the hassle of the whole matter in question and causing Mum extra washing. As if she didn't have enough on her hands! Don't go thinking though that my mother is a real bad mum, because she isn't at all like that. She can be, however, a little stern at times and lose her patience. But then who wouldn't with the next matter I'm coming to?

Most of my brothers and sisters, of which by the way I am the 14th from 16 of us; have already grown up and got married, the oldest being Amy who I think is around 37 by now, and is married to Arthur. They have been married a long time already and have a son and two daughters. I was only two when they "tied the knot". (Why folks say this I still haven't understood.) Don't remember it, the tying of this knot, of course. Amy works as a seamstress making costumes for the theatre.

I realize now that I am not the 14th from 16 of us, because originally Mum and Dad had 18 children but two of my brothers have since passed away. I reckon that's because most of the family have gone their separate ways, so to speak, and I keep forgetting who has gone where, but now I am telling you about myself I remember again. You see Charles would have been my oldest brother at 36 years old, if he was still alive that is, but he isn't here anymore and it's very sad as he was only 24 years old when he died. He worked as a quarryman at the local quarry and I was very little when he died, so I don't know what happened.

Kate, who is 34, lives just down the road from us with her husband Bert and I do vaguely remember her wedding, which happened when I was six. I had to put on this very white shirt, as I remember, and it buttoned right up underneath my chin and I could hardly breathe it was so tight. They have one son and three daughters.

Then there is my other sister Alice, who is 32 years old and went and married a 'foreigner' (according to my dad) but he isn't really, well I don't think so because we can all understand him as he talks English, but he does have a strange voice, now I come to think of it. Anyway he, his name is Charles by the way, comes from America and actually they are planning to travel there as I speak. They have four children already, and that's a mighty long way away to take them and Dad hates it something dreadful. They have all girls, by the way. First there is Daisy, Rose, then Violet and last but not least is little Ruby. I manage to remember them as they all have 'flower' names, as you might have noticed.

Arthur would have come next if he'd still been alive too. But he went and died as well when he was only 26 years old and I still can't get my head around it. He worked as a stone mason and I was 12 when he died and I don't want to talk about it. I will only say that there was heaviness in the house for ages after and it took Dad, especially, weeks and weeks to get to grips with it all.

Beatrice is in service as a lady's maid (which, now I hear myself saying that, has a certain ring about it) to a Miss Townsend down towards the south of the country in a place by the sea called Torquay. She hasn't married yet and at 29 years old, Dad says he is just waiting for it to happen. I call her 'Beatty' (always have done actually). When she comes home to visit us she has loads to say and actually we all have a hard time listening, as she does go on a bit. As a matter of fact, Mum feels quite exhausted by the time she leaves.

I think 'in service' is another annoying phrase, don't you? I mean it sounds, well I don't know, kind of military, which it is not at all. She's in no army of any kind, because I've already asked that. What it really means though is just that she's helping out a much 'better off' family. The term better off comes from Mum actually. I reckon if truth be told, it sounds like these other families just wouldn't cope without people like my sisters to go and help them. I am glad they get paid well for doing it though.

Tom was a farm labourer until he signed on for the army when he reached 18. He was away for two whole years and I reckon Dad missed him being around the village. He came back to Evercreech, of course, and has a lovely wife called Ada and two little girls, Muriel aged 3 and Lillian, who is 2. He works up at the milk and cream factory as a dairyman. John is 26 years old and he works for Mr. Allen as an assistant at the Mineral Waterworks, which is near the milk factory. He still lives with us.

Bessie, whose first name is actually Edith, but we call her Bessie, is 24 and she and Mabel left us to find 'new lives in America' (their words and not mine) more's the pity, as Mabel used to tell me all sorts of stories and I liked her company. I remember them coming to say goodbye because it was while I was working at the brickyard and me and Jesse were allowed to stay home that day, and plus that it was only last year when it happened and they had to go to a big port called Southampton.

They were heading for New York and then on to Philadelphia to stay with my Auntie Elizabeth.

Mabel is 21 now and has "*come of age*", as Mum puts it. (Mum keeps track of all our ages and writes it all down in a little notebook). I have never really understood what coming of age is supposed to mean. All I know is that every time one of us in the family reaches '21' *we've reached it!* I can't wait to reach it myself!

Fred is training in Salisbury at the moment also for the war and he is 23 years old, but he's a real scholar and Dad says he'll 'go far' when he gets out of the army. I just hope by going far, he doesn't go off to America like the others.

Ah... then comes Laura, who is 19 years old, and is sweet to me when she comes to visit us and is also in service as a servant to a very important man called Mr. Head who owns a very large house in Bournemouth. Another lucky location for her because it is within walking distance of the sea and the air is lovely and fresh, she often tells us.

Jesse is a year older than me but he is worse than me for getting-up-to-know-good. He is always doing something to make Mum go red in the face. Such as what kind of no good you might be wondering to yourselves? Let me think... like tying string to the next-door's knob and joining it to ours. You don't know the joke? Well, if you tighten it when your door is open and the other one isn't and then shut it, the other door opens... well all I know is it's funnier when you see it than it is explaining it. Also another strange habit that Jesse seems to have is that of never seeming to come home empty-handed. Bearing in mind that he mostly leaves home empty-handed, well apart from food, of which he has eaten by the time he gets to his destination, even if it be for work. He always manages to pick up something along the way and bring it home. Then he'd more than often flog it to a friend for a halfpenny.

Caroline is my younger sister, she's 14 now and Mum is kind of holding on to her a bit, so she says to Dad, as really she ought to be going 'in service' too. But she does a lot around the house like keeping it clean and washing clothes and such. She is also the only one out of all of us that has a nickname, which Mum more often than not uses. She's also called 'Queenie'. Dad explained to me, when I was old enough to understand, the reason for this. It's that Mum just happened to yell out at birth that she was the 'Queen of the Crop'.

Most of my brothers and sisters, of which by the way I am the 14th from 16 of us; have already grown up and got married, the oldest being Amy who I think is around 37 by now, and she is married to Arthur.

Then last, but certainly not least of all, is Cecil. I have just had a thought; if Caroline is 'Queenie' then shouldn't Cecil have had a nickname too; like 'Kingie' or something? Anyhow he's 12 years old and I take great pleasure in *him* looking up to me. I am like his older brother and all. He helps Dad on the farm but says he would like to be a gardener.

'Broadening' myself

Oh I know what you are probably wondering. Where the heck do we all sleep? Being as we are such a big family and all. But you see, because of the difference in our ages and most of us having already gone off to service when becoming of "a ripe enough age" (another of Dad's quotes), there were never more than eight of us at most in one bed at a time!

There were frequently four of us up one end and four down the other end of the bed, that's how it has been for us many a time.

Nobody worries though, it's just how things are and anyway its fun being all crammed into one bed, at least you manage to keep each other warm and half the time you'd be too tired to worry about giving it another thought that you're not the only one in the bed! Anyhow there is not enough room for more than one big bed. The room just wouldn't take it.

The only thing that ever bothered any one of us, would be when one of us would have to scramble out of bed, often climbing across your brother or sister, to do a jimmy riddle (as I like to call it – you know, go to the toilet in the old china pot). That would sometimes get me a giggling though or that's what my sisters used to say to me.

The worst that can happen to the one that's going to have a jimmy riddle is spilling the pot whilst carefully pulling it from under the bed or pushing it back under. I once forgot and Laura put her foot in it the next morning, which was a bit of a laugh, although she didn't think so at the time.

Not that us boys used this old china pot much, only when we were too small to know better. No us boys do the decent thing and brave the dark and cold to walk downstairs, out the door and into the outhouse. We've toughened-up. Which is another of Mum's quotes or actually that one was probably a quote from Dad. Boys are just tougher than girls!

We always had a kind of screen though which Mum opened out mornings and evenings so as the older boys and girls could dress and undress with some kind of privacy and stopping anyone from having a peep. Mum would say to me, "you'll understand when you're older my son, you'll be wanting your privacy too, mark my words". I guess I know now what she meant!

My father would say, by the time you've reached 14 and your school days are over, well you're old enough to 'broaden' yourself and earn your own keep, so to speak. And sure enough each brother and sister would do exactly that. I sure want to 'broaden' myself too.

Although he didn't mean to go and 'broaden' ourselves all the way to the United States of America as Alice and Bessie have done. Why they'd want to go so far to get a better life is quite beyond me; what's wrong with this country anyhow? Does it sound like I've disapproved of their going? Blimey, it does a bit doesn't it? I reckon Bath is as far as I'm ever going to get.

Bath is a big roman city and it takes just a train journey to get there. But I've heard it's a grand place with splendid buildings and tall houses with pillars and even houses built in half circles. I'd like to go there and that is where I am going one of these days if I have my way. When I go to 'broaden' myself that is, then I shall begin there.

Dad says the war seems to be a certain thing and is worrying about my older brothers already. He tries to encourage Jesse to work on the farm with him because he reckons that otherwise, when he is 18 years old, that he will be called up to join the war as well. But Jesse doesn't seem to worry that much, in fact Jesse never seems to worry about anything at all. I don't really like to admit it, but he is a lazy brother. Oh, he'll get up in the mornings, I don't mean that, but he'll *scarper* as soon as no-one is keeping an eye on him to ask him what he is doing today, and when he scarpers he doesn't go straight to help Dad but usually goes off up the road, getting into some kind of trouble or other. Apart from that, Jesse is a laugh and I get on really well with him. Although Dad doesn't think much of me if I let Jesse "lead me up the garden path" (a saying my mum has, which basically means just getting up to no good).

I would really like to follow in my bigger brothers footsteps though and enlist in the army.

I have already experienced several different trades. The first was when I left school and went to work for Mr. Waldo Allen who is a local builder in the village and I have been a cutter in his brick yard. Jesse has worked there too as a cutter.

Then after that job, I found a much better one driving the Reverend Dyne about the Parish in a pony and trap. That was a lovely job and I was sorry that it had to end when, after nearly a year, the poor Reverend died and I was out of a job.

I soon found another one though on the Church Farm working for Mr. Jack Welch.

I am already sixteen years old. Well actually I've just reached 16 as it was my birthday last week, 18th August, and I am well and truly a man now and feel I must do the decent thing for King and Country; well that's what the posters say. I have already seen one of them posters in Thomas Davis & Sons local grocer's window. It has this Lord Kitchener fellow pointing at you and saying you should "Join Your Country's Army" and "God save the King".

I am thinking that this King George V doesn't know who I am from *Adam*, and I can't say I know too much about him (although I have seen pictures of him and reckon my dad has a moustache just like his), but I guess it's the decent thing a man should do.

My mate says that if you join before they force you into it, that they don't check your age, otherwise you have to wait until you're at least 18 years old, when all men will be called up anyway, if it comes to it that is; and that now you get a choice of what you want to join; the navy, military or air. Later on there might not be a choice anymore. I think I'd rather be able to get to choose if I want to join, let's say, the lads on the ground, rather than on the sea. I don't much fancy being out on the sea for any length of time. My only experience of water is floating about on a lake on a raft and then I didn't much like it when I fell off and had to swim! No, a choice is good.

The only problem I find that's bothering me is how I should go about it. The "*it*" being to take my biggest steps ever towards enlisting in the Army and then working out when to take that very first step.

Should I just one day leave home and cycle off on my bike to Shepton Mallet or Castle Cary (the nearest two towns where an enlistment office is, at least that's where I imagine they are) or should I discuss the matter first with Dad?

This question I pondered about for several months on end.

I DECIDE TO ENLIST

IT'S 10TH DECEMBER AND I awaken with a realisation that I must not "think" about the matter of enlisting any further, but just go ahead and make the decision myself. It is, after all, me, Bill that has to do this. This is the one decision of my life that I must feel absolutely sure about.

If I ask Dad, he will say "wait and see, lad" because that's the way Dad thinks. If I ask Mum she will probably not like the idea at all but will be more understanding about it and would say "it's up to you dear, if you really feel that strongly about it," because that's the way Mum thinks. But then she will probably start to snivel and the snivel would turn into a sob and before I can say "bob's yer uncle" she'd be talking me out of it altogether and saying how young I am and that isn't two of her sons enough to serve King and Country? Mums can be strange like that, can't they?

I hurriedly get dressed and take a quick glance out the window to see what the weather is doing. This has been another of my stupid excuses. If it was raining or windy, until now I had just thought, 'oh maybe I won't go today but wait for better weather'. *Better weather?* Come on now Bill? What am I? A right old softy is what I've been for even thinking like that. They sure don't want any wining sissies in the army now do they? What kind of example am I setting myself, even thinking such thoughts? No, even if it's snowing today, I'm going.

Luckily for me it isn't snowing, or windy, or raining. It didn't even look cold out there. But just to be sure I pull an extra thick jumper over my head. It's no good being careless now is it? I won't be no good to anyone if I don't look after myself now will I?

I have to look the part. A decisive fellow is how I must look.

Downstairs I don't bump into Mum or see Cecil or Caroline. Good. No-one to ask me where I am going. I grab a crust of bread that I see on the kitchen table and quickly walk out the back door.

I get hold of the bicycle that's leaning against the shed and think how lucky I am that no-one else needs it at this minute, and off I go down the path and out the back gate. I take one last glance behind me to see if anyone is looking out a window or poking their head around the corner of the houses before I jump on the bike and pedal as fast as I can.

I shoot down that alleyway like water out of a plughole. A quick sharp turn to the right at the end and then a slight left turn and straight out onto Weymouth Road and a swerve to the right and I am off. I pedal past the Police Station so fast I reckon I might be caught for speeding if the Constable was about. As I pedal down the road and under the bridge I figure I might as well head for Castle Cary, as I am going in that direction.

I begin to feel good about myself. I breathe in the fresh crispiness of the air and enjoy the crust of bread, although it's got a bit squashed in my hand it tastes real good.

I reach Castle Cary in what feels like record time, but probably isn't, as I realise I am panting like a dog. 'I must work on my condition,' I think to myself, as I step off the bike and walk through the town. Now let's see where would the enlisting office be I wonder? It hadn't even occurred to me until now that maybe it would have been wiser if I'd asked in Evercreech before jumping on my bike.

I ask an old man who I pass by the duck pond. "It's opposite the old lock-up," he says to me. I thank him and keep on walking up the town towards the market hall. You see, everyone who is local around here knows what and where the old lock-up is. It's just behind the market hall and sits in the middle of the road, so to speak. It looks like a rather big police helmet built in stone and was used to lock up thieves and people who were caught up in various other petty crimes. I don't think it's used nowadays though.

Well, there is no missing the army enlisting office, as there are posters in the windows. After propping my bike up against a wall, I straighten myself, catch my breath and step inside.

The officer seated behind the desk comes across as a very kind and considerate but serious man. He asks me a few questions to find out how serious I am about joining and then what do you reckon he says to me? He says, "Well lad, to be honest the recruiting office isn't actually here. I'm just here to guide lads like you in the right direction. It's back past the duck pond, along the road, past the Primary School and up the slope, past The Park and on the left hand side is where you need to go, to the Drill Hall."

So out I come and quickly jump on my bike in the direction of the duck pond. I pass the old man and he shouts something in the way of, "that were quick me lad" and "jolly good on you". Apparently though, I can't blame the old man for his not knowing where it was, as I'm told this Drill Hall has only recently been built and not everyone who is local is aware of it.

I'm cycling like mad, working up a sweat and wishing I'd hung on to that crust of bread a little longer, when I finally realise I've passed the slope I was supposed to go up and jam on my front breaks so hard I almost fly over the handlebars. Talk about getting myself all worked up, I've now shook myself up to a right old state.

I walk the last part and try to settle myself down a bit. The last thing I'd want is to come over as a bloomin' nervous wreck!

I'm not the only lad about though as there seems to be a small queue. Which, I am grateful to, as I need the time to steady my feet and catch my breath. The man inside the office is as kind, if not kinder, than the one near the 'lock-up'. He just asks my age, where I work and a little about myself. I can hear my own voice but I feel really strange. He can tell that I am a little nervous but talks very encouragingly to me. Okay, so this is the part where I convince him that I am 17 years old and almost 18. My Dad always says "a little white lie now and then doesn't hurt anyone". Well, this was my time to tell one![1]

I explain to him about how I feel and ask if am I correct in thinking that I can choose where I will be placed. He says "you are allowed to choose from land, air or sea but not where in the country, that depends on your regiment of choice". Boy, was I relieved about that.

Of course I hadn't the faintest idea what to join, except not the Navy, but I had help and advice there at the enlisting office and was told that I couldn't go wrong by joining an infantry battalion, as they reckoned that a typical battalion spent only about 5-10 days a year in the real intense action; so, of course, I thought "well, if it comes down to it, then it won't be so bad after all". Not that I'd be a coward when it comes to action. But, let's face it, if it comes down to a choice I'd rather not fight *all* the time. Well,

[1] It was known that the expected age of recruitment was from 18 years up to about 45. Also during the recruiting, the officers were not that concerned about the ages of the boys, unless they did happen to look particularly young.

anyhow, I guess I haven't thought of the "fighting" part that much. Why look for it? That's my motto.

I have to have a physical, not that there is anything wrong with me, I'm as fit as a fiddle, and that's just what the officer said too. "Just right my lad not too skinny and not too fat. Perfect," is what he said to me. Mind you, after cycling all this way I must have had a real good colour, rosy cheeks and all!

Then he started to measure me, which got me worried a bit. I hadn't heard my friend mention this. He was checking my height. What if I'm too short, I was thinking. Then he even took my chest measurement, which was a sigh of relief, as I thought he was measuring me up for a coffin right there and then! You know, perhaps for quickness in the time of need. But no, it must be ready for the uniform.

I walked outside that door on 10th of December feeling quite proud of myself. I have never done anything remotely like this before in my life. Never needed to.

Riding my bicycle on the way back to Evercreech I had quite a knot in my stomach. For the first time in my life I had signed my name on a form and made a commitment. There was no going back. Well, I suppose there might have been, but that wouldn't be wise now would it? For a start, I would make a right fool of myself and then they would most likely realize that I *was* only 16 years old, in mind and in spirit. No, blimey, I couldn't even think about doing a thing like that. I was committed now and had to face up to it. I kept saying to myself "you've done the right thing Bill" over and over as I cycled back towards home.

I rode my bike with a certain steadiness that I hadn't had when I had made my way towards Castle Cary. I was a lot calmer now I was on my way back home. I took deep breaths of fresh air and it felt good. *I felt good.* Nervous but good. 'What are the chances of actually having to kill someone?' I suddenly thought to myself. I nearly fell of my bike thinking about *that,* so I talked myself out of even letting the thought enter my mind. I wouldn't think so much about it. I decided I would take it all in my stride, as it were, wherever I was and if it happened to come to *that,* well, I'd be prepared for it.

No, my worst problem, if I saw it as a problem, would be telling Mum and Dad. I'd have to tell them, wouldn't I? Or need I? Maybe I could just wait until the actual papers arrived through the post.

I could just imagine it now, seeing the envelope lying on the hall floor. Mum (or Dad) picking it up and looking at it. Seeing my name on the envelope. Probably an envelope with Army marks on it. Well that would give the game away, wouldn't it?

Then the shout. "*William!*" (they only call me 'William', funnily enough, if they're annoyed about something I've done).

I feel shivers all over, despite being hot from cycling! Oh no. I *must* let them know before the envelope arrives. Yes, get it over and done with right away. I'll speak to them this evening. Depending, of course, how their moods are. That's what I'll do. Whew, I feel better already!

I suddenly realised I was already outside our front gate! How did that happen? Was I aware of how I'd been cycling? "Well, stupid, course you must have been," I say to myself "or else you wouldn't have gotten here now would you?" That's scary.

Telling Mum and Dad

I WENT TO BED late. No... I decided *not* to tell them this evening. Mum was tired and Dad was grumbling about something Jesse had done, or not done.

I couldn't seem to sleep. I went downstairs and out the back door towards the outhouse. I was just about finishing relieving myself of a very long pee when Cecil tapped my shoulder. I turned with such a fright, still peeing, and soaked the poor little chap behind me! "What d'je goes and do that for?" I asked Cecil. He was stood in front of me holding a candle in his right hand. Boy, did he look frightened.

"Blimey, you're jumpy aint je?" I didn't bother to answer him, but quickly grabbed the first thing I put my hand on and tried mopping up the mess on the floor.

"Damn it Bill, you do realize that you've only gone and peed on me, don't you?"

"Well sorry, but serves you right for creeping up on me like that."

I wasn't in the mood for talking and brushed past him and walked down the path. I washed my hands in the kitchen and crawled back upstairs to bed.

After breakfast the next morning, there I am on my bicycle pedaling up the village street to the local doctor. The assistant says she can 'squeeze me in' if I can wait five minutes or so. This I can do, I tell her. Gosh, I feel quite the much older for this already! Making decisions; seeing the doctor by myself. What's next? I haven't seen our doctor for a very long time, never needed to and I don't even know his name. So, when it is my turn to go in and he looks up and sees me, he is quite taken aback.

"William Ralph Upshall, take a seat lad. Haven't seen you since you were knee high to a grasshopper!" Well that broke the ice. Why do people say that? What does it mean?

Anyhow, at first he is rather worried about me. Am I sure this is what I want to be doing? Have I thought this through and why the hurry?

But after talking for some time he comes to a decision to agree to do the physical if I agree to talk to Mum and Dad as soon as I get back.

It's just as I thought too. I'm as fit as a fiddle! "Not too skinny and not too fat," says doc, just like they said in Castle Cary. He gives me a bit of advice too. He reckons I should eat well and build up my strength before I get 'called up' and explains that army food is good but not like your mum's home cooking, if I know what he means by that. I agree and say that I'll do my best.

Nothing much happened for a couple of weeks after, just the day to day normality, but then our worst fears struck. Alice came for a visit with her four children. Alice explained that she and Charles had both made the decision to move to America. They were going to a place called Connecticut, where Charles grew up and have decided to make it their family home. Charles had already left for America to arrange matters and Alice and the children were to follow on 30th September from Liverpool.

Mum and Dad had half been expecting this day to come but now it had they wish it hadn't, if that makes any sense at all. As you can imagine, there were many tears and hugs and kisses. We all wished them all the best and to mind they keep in touch and wished them a very safe journey. What a day that was.

It's Boxing Day and I have decided that today I shall tell Mum and Dad my bit of 'news'. What? Okay so it's taken me more than a few days to break the news. I just haven't been able to pick the right moment, that's all. Well, maybe that and *pluck up* the courage. But, hey, today is the day. Well, I couldn't tell them yesterday, now could I, even if they were all in good spirits? I just couldn't be the one to spoil their Christmas now could I? And you might be thinking to yourselves, "Well, Bill, what makes today any different?" I don't know the answer to that. All I know is that this morning we're all going up to the village cross and gather for the "hunt", so I reckon it's as good a time as any.

By the "hunt" I mean the Foxhunt, which is every year on Boxing Day and all the horses and hounds meet at the Bell Inn. They wait there until all participants have arrived and after they have had their 'hot toddy' for the warm up, they set off through the village and out into the countryside to start the chase. We all gather around the village cross because it has more space and, if you are small, you can climb up the cross steps to get a better view, depending on the village crowd that is. Its good weather so there probably will be a crowd watching.

We get there at 10.30. At 11 o'clock the leader of the hounds blows his horn and they're off. It's great. I wish I could ride a horse. But then, that would be no use because you need to actually have a horse of your own to ride and we don't have that kind of money.

When the crowd thins out, Mum and Dad make their way towards the Bell Inn. Dad usually likes to treat himself to a pint of cider with Mum afterwards. As we are walking towards the Inn, I get up real close to Dad and start to talk. You see why I've also waited until now is because Tom and Fred have come to watch the hunt too. Tom is now a 'reservist' and Fred is still in the army, so that means I have a lot of moral support to back me up here.

By the time we've reached the entrance to the bar, Dad has not only given me his approval but also a big, fat pat on the back and tells me how proud he is and that he hadn't realised how grown up I'd become all of a sudden. Well, what a turn up for the books this is! Here I've been, for days on end, figuring my brains out how best to tell him and he just accepts it. Just like that! I can't believe my ears. Maybe when it's sunk in, he'll have second thoughts.

I decide to go off down the lane with Jesse and Cecil for a while. I'd already had the sense to ask Tom to talk to Mum and Dad a bit more about the idea and soften them up a bit. But now I'm thinking well maybe I was all worked up about nothing. Perhaps he'd been expecting it to come. It's just come a little bit earlier that's all.

Jesse thinks I've gone stark raving mad and says he'll not be enlisting. He'll just wait and see if he gets called up next year, he says.

Cecil isn't too happy about me going off either. He says he'll miss me a lot when I'm gone and that it's not fair that I would even want to leave them and hadn't there been enough of our family leaving just lately?

I encourage him a bit by saying that it'll mean he'll get more chores to do and, next to Jesse, will be Dad's right hand man. He perks up, of course, after hearing me say that, and off we go across the field.

All in all it's been a great Christmas this year, I must say. I wonder what next year will bring.

The Wait

I won't bore you with the rest of my 'normal' happy-go-lucky day-to-day life. As a matter of fact, the only excitement I am now looking forward to is confirmation of my "enlisting" in the army in the first place.

As the days turn into months I am beginning to wonder if I have dreamt the whole thing. I begin to question myself as to whether they really said that I could join or whether I had been taken seriously or not. But then I remembered very clearly that I *had* signed a paper and had *definitely* made a commitment on that December day last year. I would never forget that day. Why? It just happened to be the most important day of my life. I probably said so at the time but I can't quite remember.

Mum is also beginning to notice me getting anxious. Well, she can't help but notice, as I will practically leap at her if I catch eyes on her with any post in her hands. I nearly knocked her down one day as we both got to the front door, so anxious am I.

❖ ❖ ❖

1914

Winter came and went. So did the spring. By this time I had promised myself to immediately stop waiting for post. Mum said better to forget it and then one day it will just come. Dad kept questioning my anxiety. "What's the hurry lad? The war hasn't started yet anyway. So just calm down. If it's meant to be, it's meant to be. Quit yer worrying right here and now and put more of that energy in yer work lad." He's right, of course. So I did.

Naturally when Mum had her visits on Mothering Sunday from all my sisters, who were allowed home from service to do just that and came to smother Mum with flowers and little goodies, I couldn't help but tell them of my forthcoming adventure.

I was frowned upon at first. Isn't that just typical of women? They don't seem to understand how we men think nowadays and that this was my chance to do my bit. You know, the usual things were said: "you're too young, Willie". I hate it when Amy calls me that, it's quite belittling and I told her so too. With which she promptly bit on her lip and excused herself for forgetting how old I had become.

It went a bit quiet when Alice, Bessie and Mabel were missed amongst the family gathering, but that soon was brushed under the mat, so to speak, when cakes were handed around.

I got squashed to pieces when each one of them left to return to their duties, with a reminder to stay in touch with Mum and Dad once I had left.

The envelope arrives

Then one afternoon, the 20th July, when I came home from work and opened the back door, I saw an envelope lying on the kitchen table. I walked up to it and saw a *Somerset Light Infantry* stamp in the left-hand corner of the envelope. My hands were all sweaty and that old knot in my stomach came back. I turned to wash my hands at the sink, then decided I'd freshen up completely before I touched the envelope, so I pulled off my shirt and washed my face and neck too. Then I decided to go change into clean clothes, so I went upstairs.

You guessed it, I was stalling! Here was the thing I'd waited all of seven months for. Now it had arrived I found myself hesitating. What was I hesitating for? I don't know.

I run downstairs and into the kitchen. It's still lying there on the table. I pour myself a cup of milk and pull up a chair, sit and stare at it.

"It aint gonne open by itself Bill, wha' be affeard of?"

"Blimey Mum, you scared the life out of me." Mum had glided in through the back door so quietly, I hadn't heard her and she was stood behind me.

"Well, that's 'cause you're a dreaming, lad. G'wain en open it. You've waited long enough aven't you? Wha' be a thinking lad? Ooh arr, it's got the better of ya, aint it? Ya can't pluck up the courage to open it, now can ya?" She gave me a pat on the back and came and sat opposite to me.

I picked up the envelope and handed it to her. "Open it for me, Mum, please." So she did.

She sat there and read it. Looked at me, frowned, said "Oie" and "Oh my" and I couldn't take the suspense anymore, so I snatched it right out of her hand and she frowned, looked at me and frowned again and got up out of her chair and walked around the table towards me.

I read it. "Mum! You gave me a bit of a fright there, 'cause I thought I hadn't been accepted, but I have. Why did you do that?"

"Because..." she turned around from the kitchen sink and looked at me, rubbing her hands over her apron, "ave ya seen when you've got to leave?"

I read the letter again. I had to be in Bath on the 20th of July, which was next week, Friday. (Actually it wasn't really a letter as such but more of a general army form with here and there the necessary details written in by hand).

"Next Friday, Mum. Yes, I'm off to Bath next week to join the Army". Bath of all places; didn't I say that I wanted to go to Bath? Blimey. I couldn't help it, I was smiling, I was so pleased.

"Come 'ere, lad," Mum gave me a big hug and kissed me on the cheek.

"I must go and tell Dad," I said.

"He'll be 'ome d'reckley," she replied.

I ran out the back door to find Dad and tell him. I heard what Mum had said but I couldn't wait for him to get home. I still had the letter in my hand.

Of course for the next few days Mum was in a fluster; first of all looking through my underwear with a 'fine-tooth comb' (as she put it) making sure it was all intact, then inspecting all my pairs of socks, just in case of holes which would, if found, have to be neatly darned. The letter did state though that I wouldn't need many clothes, as I would be issued with the suitable army outfit on arrival.

Not only did Mum have the worry of good underwear and such, but also of what to put them in! We didn't possess many cases. We couldn't afford much of a holiday and rarely went anywhere for a long period at a time, so cases, they weren't really a thing we owned much of. "I don't need anything large," I said to Mum, "anything that'll hold some clothes is fine by me." What she did find, she said was too tatty to send me off with but she reckoned she'd find a solution somehow. She would 'ask around' she said.

Meanwhile, I went around doing my normal chores at the farm. Mr. Welch reckoned it was mighty brave of me to jump in straight away but he said he admired me for doing so. I also found myself walking for ages around the village. I figured that if I was going to be 'away' for a while (who knows how long?) I would store as many pictures in my brain as possible. If you think that's rather sentimental for a boy like me, you'd be right in one way, but then again not. You see, I did have a sentimental streak about me. "A day-dreamer" is what my teacher would say and probably most of my family too.

Dad was quiet these last few days, I noticed. But he did say he'd be seeing me before I could say 'Jack Robinson'. (This was another of those phrases that were frequently used around these parts of the country). He thought the war might not come to much in any way and if it did it wouldn't take long before it was ended. His words not mine. "Spec you'll be 'ome in no time," he said to me.

Preparing to go

It was now the day before I was due to be in Bath. Mum had sure enough found me a suitable case, which she explained, when I'd asked where that came from, that Dad had been able to 'borrow' it from the Luff family. (They are the farmers where he works). This information was something I'd rather not have known, because it most likely meant that now this was a take-the-most-greatest-care-of-not-to-lose-it case! It looked brand new, not a scratch on it, which was even worse for me, as I had enough on my 'plate' as it was. I had much preferred a scruffy-looking case, which I'm sure I could have found lying around somewhere. But what could I do? Mum looked very proud of herself when she showed it to me and inside it looked so neat and tidy. On the outside she had tied a brown label to the handle, with my full name and address on the one side and on the other she had written the name and address of the headquarters in Bath, which was very thoughtful, I thought. "Just in case you be forgettin' to carry it off the train, me son," she said. As if I would do such a thing.

It's the 25th of July and I'm to go to headquarters in Lower Bristol Road, Bath. I am in the Somerset Light Infantry Company, the 4th Battalion. Finally I get to go to Bath! Didn't I just reckon I'd get to go to Bath and broaden myself someday? Well there you go. Is that fate or what. Bath – here I come. I felt good. Nervous, but good.

The funny thing too, is that I hardly have to go very far to get on a train to Bath. You see just down Backway Lane from our cottage, along Weymouth Road, turn right passed Windy Farm and up an embankment to the small Evercreech New Station. Isn't that convenient for me? Even though Evercreech is a small Somerset village, it does have its own little Railway Station. In fact, Evercreech has two Stations; I feel like I am boasting a bit now, but the other Station is virtually just about a mile down the road, up a hill and you are at the Evercreech Junction Station. So, my small village is really quite well-known, if you are a train!

Blimey, here I go then, off to Bath to join the Army. I decided to walk down towards Weston Town (the road that follows Weymouth Road) to call in and say goodbye to Amy before leaving and then I made my way under the railway bridge and I climbed the small stone steps up the embankment. As I get up high on the bank directly across the railway line from me I find myself staring at two fine looking horses. They happen to be from the Lime Kiln, which is directly below on the other side. Now I'll just tell you a funnier sight; if you were stood on the road and you were looking upwards at the horses, well, they'd look as if they're stood on the rooftop. Which in a way would be correct, but it's just the access way which slopes up from the Kiln.

Along the railway line and a little walk further takes me to the station building where I buy a one-way ticket to Bath (Queen Square) Park Station. I have to buy a one-way ticket as; of course, I don't know when I'll be back. It does feel kind of strange though, buying a ticket and no return!

Mum and Dad, and Jesse, Caroline, Cecil and even Laura have all come and are stood ready and waiting for me. They walked on in front of me you see. They said they wanted to give me 'a send off' so to speak. Although it was a nice surprise to see Laura I must admit, I hadn't expected her to be here too. This send-off was fine by me. We did exactly the same for Fred, Tom and John. I kind of feel like I'm emigrating or something just like Mabel and Bessie did.

I don't have to wait too long. We can see the steam approaching us as it gushes out over the bushes along the railway track even before we see the train. "Ere she comes lad," shouts Dad. Here's where the butterflies start cracking in inside my stomach. "She sure looks grand, so she does lad." Dad loves his trains. "Come here quick me lad and give us a grand old hug before anyone on the train sees us." Dad knows by now that I don't like too much of a fuss. All that kissing and hugging at my age is somewhat embarrassing. He respects me for that. But I make an exception just for today and give everybody a big hug back.

"Now, Bill, 'ave you got yer ticket ready?" says Mum. "Yes Mum, here it is."

"Now, yer know whirr to get off the train, don't you? You've got directions from the station to Lower Bristol Road. I tucked em in yer inside coat pocket for ya, so as not to get lost, Bill." Mum's a bit nervous by now and is that a tear I see running down her cheek? I pull out my nice clean white handkerchief from my inside pocket and wipe away her tears.

"Oh now, Bill, watch what yer a doing!" She picks up my piece of paper with the directions on it. It must have fallen out my pocket when I pulled out the handkerchief. "You be careful now not to lose that again, now won't you Bill?" She keeps saying my name (a sign of nervousness). "Don't be spuddling along yer way." 'Spuddling' is a bit of a slang word for causing trouble. As if I would be doing that at any point.

I straighten myself up, pick up my borrowed case, and board the train. I take a seat next to a window, facing towards the direction of Bath (I hate sitting backwards). Anyhow the train is not that busy yet.

Hello, what's Dad doing? Dad has jumped on board the train and is coming towards me. Have I dropped something else, I wonder. "Come ere, me lad," he says, and crouches over me for one more hug. "You're off on the 'slow and dirty' and I'm downright proud of ya Bill. But you be taking care of yourself now, you hear me." The train whistle blows.

"Dad, quick jump off the train or you'll be coming with me."

We each give a grin and he's gone.

On the train to Bath

I wave frantically as the train pulls away from Evercreech New Station, off on my trip to Bath and the Army.

The 'slow and dirty' that my Dad mentioned was the name given to these trains, especially trains going towards Bath. The journey can be, at times, slow and the dirty part, well that refers more to the amount of smoke that will come out of one of these trains when they have to climb a hill or go under a tunnel. In other words – you don't want to stick your head out the window during those times!

I just open the window a little for the fresh air. There is nothing worse than a stuffy carriage. I suddenly remember the Prestleigh Viaduct, so I stand up and cross over to the other side to get a good look. I have seen this viaduct before, of course, but can never get enough of it. What is it exactly, this viaduct? Well it is basically a long bridge stretching between the hills and it stands high over the fields below, but what makes it special are the arches. I'm not sure how many there are, strangely enough I've never bothered to count them. But these curved arches (in fact there are 11, I've just counted them!) well they just make you want to gasp for joy.

They are like railway monuments. I love to look at them and now, I'm travelling over them, and it makes it even more exciting. I don't get to go on a train that often. It's quite expensive for us so we only get to go on special occasions, like Christmas, when we go to into Shepton Mallet to see the Christmas decorations. Actually I think its better that way. It keeps it special.

Getting back to the viaduct, I just remembered that Dad has told me that the next viaduct after Prestleigh has even more curved arches, about 27 or more I think. Also it's the longest of the viaducts in this area, as I recall.

How does my dad know all of this? Ah, now here's the thing. You see, before Dad worked at the farm, he used to work for the railway company as I did mention in the beginning. When his work was done he would often walk the line or sit on a bank and watch the trains pass by. This Evercreech to Bath railway line in particular means a lot to him. To be able to say that you've worked on something as grand as a railway really makes a difference to a lot of people. I've never really thought of it like that, but now, just sitting here with time to think, I realize just how great my dad is and what he has done in his lifetime already. Now I understand why he would want to tell me this. Why shouldn't he? And another thing, he gave up his old home farm in Dorset many years ago just for that purpose. *Blimey*, if I can do something as equally important as what my dad has done, I sure would be real pleased with myself too.

Oh, hang on. The train is reaching Shepton Mallet Station, so I'd better get back to my take-the-most-greatest-care-of case before anyone gets on. I sure don't want to lose it already. I must stop myself from worrying too much about this stupid case. It's just a case and I certainly will not lose it.

I wonder if any of these men are off to join the army too. I wish I was more forward, but I'm not, so I stare out the window again once we set off to enjoy more scenery.

We are on to the Mendips now. The Mendips are high hills and I hear the train as it puffs away pulling itself, and us, up these hills. Let me think. What did Dad used to say? A one in fifty gradient or even one in seventy, or something to that amount, is what some of these hills have. If you understand your gradients you'll imagine how steep this is and what it must be like for this poor old train to get us up and over! I kind of feel sorry for the train.

When I was younger I used to think that trains could talk. Well, you know what I mean, if you listen to their noises and their puffs of steam, it's like they are telling us how difficult they've got it. Or when they are travelling along fast, when it's nice and straight, it's like they're pleased with themselves. Am I sentimental or what? I can't help it.

I hope I'm tough enough for this army? Who am I kidding; I *can be* tough when I want to be. Sure I can. Or should I say when I'll *have* to be.

I think I must have dosed off a bit. We seem to have more passengers. What have I missed? My case. Where's my borrowed take-the-most-greatest-care-not-to-loose-it case gone?

Oh God, now don't get panicky or you'll make a scene, I think to myself.

"Looking for your brown case lad?" says a chap across from me. "Don't you worry; I've put it in the rack above your head for now, it'll be safer up there out the way of everybody." I then realized there was also a man sat next to me reading a paper.

"Thank you sir. I have to take care of it. I've borrowed it you see." What's wrong with me? Why should I be telling him that I've borrowed it? What a nightmare. I'm getting myself all-of-a-twist about this stupid case again.

The man smiles at me. Can he see that I'm a bit new to travelling and that I might be a touch nervous? Oh you bet he can. It's probably written all over my face. *Come on Bill what's got into you. Pull yourself together here, this instant.* (Words my mum would probably be saying to me right now). Sometimes I am positive that she can read my mind.

"Off somewhere important are we lad?"

I tell him, "Well yes sir, I'm on my way to Army Headquarters at Bath." Well, that's important enough for me.

"Good for you my lad!" He says.

Well now I feel tons better.

I wanted to ask him where he was headed but thought the better of it. Mum always said that you shouldn't impose on grown-ups and to mind your own business.

"In fact, that's exactly where I'm also heading. What a coincidence, don't you agree?" There you go. He's told me himself anyhow. I smile just a little bit and think to myself how fortunate I am in sitting near him. All I need do in Bath is follow him.

Well, that's if he heads straight to the Headquarters. I mean, wouldn't it be silly of me if I were to just follow him and not take note of where I am going and land up at someone's house, or such. No, perhaps it won't be wise of me to just assume he'll go straight there. I will take notice of my note that Mum carefully jotted down for me. Hmm, yes better to do that. It'll look better, even if he is heading straight there. He'll think I'm more sensible that way.

Oh, tunnel coming. That means we're at Winsor Hill. Now we're in complete darkness. Luckily it's just for a short while. I've never much liked going into tunnels. Jesse and Caroline have always thought them fun and exciting and they'd get a kick out of them if they were here right now. I should feel the same, but I don't. I feel unsafe in a tunnel. It's dark for a second or two. Who knows what can happen in a second or two. I know, I'm a dramatic. But come on, you never can tell. Take for instance this man sat next to me. He's been quiet all this time. Reading. But who knows, he might suddenly grab his chance in the darkness to take flight with, let's say, my case! Well now wouldn't that be just my bad luck. Okay, it's highly unlikely, but something else he might do. Something even worse. I'm just guessing, of course.

He doesn't though. We're all safe.

We are approaching Masbury Station now. Although it's small, I like this station as it's different to normal stations. On the platform is the stationmaster's house with a bay window. It has this fancy carving of a mediaeval castle, the Maesbury Castle. And there was actually an iron-age fort here once. Just imagine living in a castle. Wow, now that would be exciting!

25TH JULY 1914 - ARRIVAL AT LOWER BRISTOL ROAD, BATH

"HEY, HELLO LADDY, WAKE up. We're approaching Bath." Ugh, what, umm, did I just doze off or what? Blimey, am I lucky this man is kind enough to wake me up. I can't believe I fell asleep again like that. I thank him. The other man that was sat next to me wasn't there anymore. He must have gotten off somewhere along the way. How long have I been asleep? And all the while I'm wondering about this, the kind man has already stood up to lift down my case.

Thank god that's still safe and sound. Well, that's a laugh, I suddenly feel really stupid, as my take-the-most-greatest-care-not-to-lose-it- suitcase, could jolly well have been a lost case! I mean anyone could have taken a fancy to it and grabbed it while I was sleeping. Unless, of course, the kind man stopped them first. Unless that.

I look out the window and see that we're just coming into Bath Park Station. I swallow a lump in my throat. It looks big. Big, but grand is Queen Square Station. We grind to a halt. There are a lot of people out there. I turn to find that the kind man has already disappeared. Where'd he go so quickly? I grab for my case and walk to the open door and step down onto the platform.

I find a quiet spot to take it all in and look around. The kind man is nowhere to be seen. Well, there goes my theory of following him anywhere! I realise that my bladder could do with emptying so I decide that I'd better get that sorted first.

Phew, that's better. Boy did I need that! It must have been the excitement of it all as I haven't drunk anything at all yet. They were some posh lavatories too I might add.

I'm just about to put my case on the ground when a crowd of chaps come towards me. Perhaps I'd better keep hold of it, I think to myself. I struggle to find my piece of notepaper with Mum's directions on it. Ah, here it is. Now, let me see what she's written:

My dearest Bill,

Now lad mind you watch your back now and keep a hold a that ther suitcase. Now Bill when you walk out a that station you take a left and a left again and walk towards the main road. That'll be the lower Bristol road. It might be marked up, then again it might not. Cross over to'ther side a that road and walk to your left. You ave to go a while down the road and twill be somewhere on the right that you gotta turn into. Any how's I'm sure it'd be marked from there on. You be sure and ask otherwise. Use that tung in yer head now mind. Don't be gettin shy.

Love you lots son.

Mind you keep in touch.

xx Mom. xx

Well, that note near enough brings tears to my eyes.

When Mum writes something down, well, she just writes what she's thinking and sometimes it comes out real funny like now. My mum and my dad too come to that, talk a lot of Somerset dialect and I reckon I do too, but perhaps not quite as much as them. Kind of brings a smile to your face doesn't it?

Anyhow, I mustn't stand here idling my time away. Let's go find this place.

With Mum's note held firmly in my right hand and my case in my left I walk towards the station exit and out onto the streets of Bath.

I follow Mum's instructions and soon enough I am walking along the Lower Bristol Road. I soon notice that I don't seem to appear to be the only chap walking this very same road. I see walking in front of me several others and I decide to catch up with them and, yes, I do manage to put my mind to it and speak to them, asking if they just so happen to be looking for the Headquarters too, as that's where I am heading.

"Yes," they say all at once, with much excitement. I push Mum's note into my trouser pocket. I won't need this now.

After what seemed like ages we find a right-hand turn into a smaller lane with a sign announcing *Army Headquarters*. We all follow each other and sure enough just up this lane we meet more chaps and men in uniform.

When we got as far as the headquarters we could see a whole gathering of chaps talking to each other. We found out that before going inside (a side entrance) we had to state our name. They wanted to check us all individually. Wouldn't want any intruders going into a place like this. *Especially* a place like this, I was thinking. I can understand that. And this *is* the army after all. They probably check and recheck everything. So I went to join the rest in the queue.

Before long I wasn't at the end of this queue either. Where did they just come from? I noticed many of these chaps were holding their letters in their hands. *Blimey*, I thought, where's mine. Have I got it with me? I didn't know whether I should stand here and look for it while I've got the chance, or should I just hope they won't ask me for it, when it's my turn. Not everyone was holding their letter, so I decided to just wait and see. No way was I going to bend over in this queue and start opening up my case!

It's my turn.

"Name?"

"William Ralph Upshall," I say with as much enthusiasm to it as I could muster. He's looking down his list of names, turns a page and finds it.

"Next," he calls and I look around and see another man in uniform beckoning me to step inside.

I find myself in a large, open room filled with men and lads chattering away and asking each other questions. The noise, well, it reminded me of an assembly room at school. At first I just stood there and didn't know what to do. It felt awkward. I felt awkward. Just the same feeling you get when you start the next school and are the new boy. But surely all these chaps were new boys and men too? I decided to stand near another chap who just happened to look as lost as me and hope that we might strike some conversation up between us.

It worked! We got talking and he said his name was A.J. Just that. Apparently he liked to be called by his initials, which I thought odd at the time. Maybe he had a very peculiar name.

After some while we were all led into another large room. We were all welcomed to Bath and thanked with loads of appreciation for making the very important choice of enlisting in the army. The talks and speeches went on and on and, quite frankly, was a lot to take in for me. In fact the minutes turned into hours, it seemed, and was very tiresome. For some time thereafter everything seemed a blur. Like when you know you're taking part in something, but actually feel like you're somewhere else too. I think somewhere along the way we were shuffled into groups.

There was so much talking. I am not used to all of this. It made me feel if I had done the right thing. This was the first time that I begun to feel claustrophobic, and was really pleased when I somehow managed to escape with A.J. out a side door for a moment for a breath of fresh air. We'd kind of stuck by each other's sides during this whole new experience. He said I had gone really as white as a sheet. I said that he looked white too and we laughed for the first time.

All this time I still had hold of my take-the-most-greatest-care-not-to-loose-it suitcase!

Next we were shown where our sleeping quarters were. Another large room. Upstairs though this time. There were rows of beds. As soon as we were allowed to pick a bed, I just walked to the nearest, I mean a bed is a bed right? They all were exactly the same, except that some were close by a window. And I was thankful to let go of my suitcase.

Combat Uniform

Quite frankly, it all became too much for me after this to take in and by the time we were allowed to go to bed, I was exhausted and everything around me seemed to be humming and the room was kind of hazy.

Blimey, what a day! I don't even remember undressing!

We were all told that we could expect to stay here for at least a fortnight.

Although my surroundings were now different and many of the chaps were still chatting to each other, I had no trouble whatsoever in falling asleep.

What's all the noise? It's like waking up in a classroom. Everyone's dressing like mad and rushing about and talking of breakfast. Well I've saved a bit of time in that respect as I am already dressed! A.J. who must have parked himself next to me laughed and said I'd just keeled over and that was about it. Fast asleep!

I'm famished. All I need is to find the toilet, freshen up and I'm ready to go.

Down the stairs and along a corridor was the breakfast area. This was like walking into a very large canteen with row upon row of long tables and benches and chaps stuffing themselves with toast.

I found the end of the queue and before long had grabbed a mug of tea and a pile of toast! Where to sit? I found an end of a bench and plonked myself down, which seemed to automatically send a ripple of shifting up and shuffling along to make more elbow room, which was good. I could get used to this.

I won't bore you with a lot more detail of the daily routine, but the next real exciting day, was the day we were issued with our army uniform. None of us could wait for this day. Well, now let's be honest. You join the army for the good of it and yourself doing your bit for King and country, but, apart from the exercises and the running about getting fit, you do want to wear that all important uniform. It's what makes you feel a part of it all.

We finally got issued with our "Combat uniform", (I do like the sound of that). Combat. That's a great word.

I also got to carry a gun as part of my equipment, which makes sense, of course, but when I got to collect mine with the rest of us chaps it did feel incredible. I mean this is a *real gun* and it's quite heavy. *Blimey*. No, we hadn't had ammunition to go with it, but then, that would be asking for trouble now wouldn't it? Especially with us trigger happy chaps. The bayonet is pretty lethal looking too.

There were lads that would keep picking it up and pointing it and making jokes and talking about the enemy and blowing out their brains and all sorts of crazy things. But this is not a game anymore is it? It's probably going to happen and I might need to use this gun. How am I supposed to feel? I have no idea. But I am putting it straight back in my cupboard for now, or until we need it for practice or whatever. I don't really want to think about *that part* at all. *Blimey*.

What I have to get used to at the moment, is the Combat uniform. The tunic, as it's called. I'd call it a jacket myself. Is of a thick woollen material and is a dark khaki colour (actually everything is khaki). That's for our benefit in the field as camouflage. The thing is about the tunic is that it itches. We've been told that everyone finds this in the beginning, but that we'll soon get used to it once we've worn it regularly and it's had some wear! Well, I hope so. There are two breast pockets and two lower pockets. On the shoulder area are straps with brass buttons. The brass buttons I do like a lot. I wonder if we are expected to keep them so shiny. More than likely we do have to. Then there are the pants with putties! What in heaven's name are putties you want to know? Well, they are strips of khaki cloth which we have to wrap around our lower legs and ankles. They do have a purpose so we've been told. They are meant to support and protect the lower half of our legs. Handy if you are riding a bicycle or horse!

Oh, and then we have our ammunition boots. They have hobnail soles. Also they are black. They are very heavy and that's because of the steel plate on the heel and the steel toecaps. This is yet another part of the uniform to get used to. Imagine having to march miles in these.

The part of the uniform that I like the best though, is the hat. Oh, mustn't say hat, so I've been told. No, it's a stiffened peak cap. It's of the same material as the tunic and also the same colour. There is a leather strap going around it with a brass fitting and the strap is secured to the cap with two small brass buttons.

As I have now my 'kit', there is no need for my 'civilian' clothes, or the take-the-most-greatest-of-care-not-to-loose-it suitcase which I came with. (Well that'll be a relief and a load off my mind!) These are to be returned to whence they came, so to speak. In other words, they are to be sent off to my home address. I have written a letter to Mum and Dad, telling them all about where I have been staying these last two weeks. That I have been talking and minding my manners and have made a friend. I reassure her that I shall be just fine and not to worry about me and I put this letter inside my case for Mum to find when she opens it up.

I hope this case doesn't get scratched on its way 'home'. I almost feel like wrapping something over it, but decide that is just silly. I have my own bag now anyway; it's called a rucksack.

Army Rules and Regulations

The days go quick and chaotic. I feel as if I'm living life in the fast lane, and it's also just like I am back at school too. But not a regular school, but like one of them boarding schools that I used to hear about back home. Where you would go if you are well-off or, if you are at the other end of the scale, and are sent to one of those workhouses or orphaned. Yes, I kind of feel like we are all orphans trying to get a grip of a new life under army command.

I will say that we do get enough of just about everything though. We have daily exercises to do out in the grounds.

Feet placing sideways
Head turning
Arms stretching upward
Arms forward and bend
Arms flinging
Bending forward
Arms stretching sideways
Heels raising, knees bending quickly

Well I won't go on and on, but that's a small insight of what we have to do to exercise. When we first begun, there was giggling and there were whispers of 'is he serious?' But none of us do that anymore. Especially when we all realised how much we ached at night and the next morning. We were using parts of our muscles that we didn't even know we had. Some chaps were feeling this more than others.

Then there were the talks. Or should I say *lessons*, yes I think that's more appropriate. A Lieutenant-Colonel someone or other, sorry I've not jotted down his name and I can't think for the life of me what it is, talked to us on a weekly basis.

Let me explain a few of his lessons to you, because they are very important and have made me look at life in a very different light.

For example I had never thought of my skin as being a covering for my protection and for getting rid of water. Which, by the way we do, by sweating. That our sweat is full of impurities and must be removed and if not removed it will be left impure and offensive. I guess by offensive, he means we'd smell.

We should wash the following every day when possible:

Between the legs and buttocks

The feet and toes

The armpits

He then lets us know that this can be done at any time of the day when we have a spare quarter of an hour!

I must admit I felt impure right there and then, not having done this even at home on a daily basis. A bath once a week is all we in our family could muster.

To frequently wash our underclothing. Not to wear the same underclothes day and night. We must also have two pairs of socks in use; one in the mornings and one in the evenings.

The next bit sticks like glue in my brain, because it made me smile.

Your boots, socks and feet should have as much attention as your rifle.

By this I think he's saying how important they are to us, this, when I think about it, is very true. Especially when you consider all the marching we're going to be doing.

Oh yes, and then the business of dirt.... Dirt doesn't exist in nature. It becomes only *dirt* when it is in the wrong place. And there's me thinking of our garden at just about this time. But then I suppose in the garden is where it should be and stay. It takes me back to thinking of Mum, yelling at us about bringing *it* inside the house and not wiping our feet by the front or back door.

Also that sand on the seashore is clean. But if the sand gets into our rifles it then also turns into dirt and it must be removed.

Our refuse and waste that we accumulate about us and gets into our homes is most dangerous and the worst form of dirt and a main cause of disease.

I must admit I am learning more right here and now than even I did at School.

Do you know we have also been told how to clean our teeth! Explaining how we should use plenty of water. Our chalk powder is just assisting in the work of cleaning, but a brush and plenty of water is all that's really necessary. Could they be letting us know that if we do run out of our chalk-powder, not to panic about it because we still have water? Better make sure the water bottles are always full though.

Oh this is another good point made aware to us: the air we breathe is the most important and is the 'breath of life'. Now that is poetry right there. We need it night and day. No kidding!

Oh, wait a minute.... windows in the barracks should be open all day and at least three inches at night. To remind us all that whoever stated that night air was harmful, was talking utter nonsense. At home Mum always kept our window open at night anyhow. I've never heard anyone mention that it might be harmful. Of course, I'm forgetting that I am used to country air and not city air. That's probably what the army means. I have no problems with this bit. I am all for having fresh air. I'd have no trouble sleeping out in the open even. I wonder if I should tell them this. No... best keep that to myself.

The talk seemed to last forever and, well, between you and me I found myself nearly nodding off! So I would advise you all to stay 'chaste'. And I am saying this for your own sakes too. Then he went on to say that we all must use self control and that it should be practised at all times. I heard this and found myself muttering "My brothers used to chase me all the time. I'm used to being chased". There were some giggles.

Did we have to let people search for us? What does he mean? Then he is talking about catching syphilis. "Catching Phyllis who?"

I am very confused. It must have been 'written all over my face' too.

A.J. nudges me with his elbow right in my side. "Bill, be quiet, he's talking about sex". Oops, that was embarrassing I can tell you! Ever have the feeling that you are turning into a beetroot?

Well I did that at that moment. I could feel the blood whooshing into my face. I was on fire. We country folk seemed to have the raw end of the deal. And raw I felt. After that little talk, it was obvious to the chaps when we went to bed that night, that some of us lads that came from out of town had less or no experience in the matter of staying *chaste* at all! My head feels like its spinning. I bet I'll never live this down. It will haunt me throughout my stay here now. Then a thought came into my head; this must be what Dad meant when he always said his sons and daughters had to go off to 'broaden yourself'. Now it's happening to me.

The talks went on and on. Water was brought up again as being the best drink. If we were not sure of it being pure enough to drink, to then boil it.

I was getting teased at breakfast for minding to watch out that I remain chaste. And, 'watch your back now Bill'. And, have I seen Phyllis lately? Little things like that. But do you know what? I took it on the chin (as Dad would have told me). I stayed focused and didn't let it bother me one bit. A bit of teasing was quite normal in the army, I'd noticed.

Off to Camp at Salisbury Plain

The days just fly by and I don't know whether I'm coming or going at the moment. Well, I do know that we are going. It's to be our first major big march. Rumours are bussing around that we are moving to a camp near Salisbury Plain.

We are called the 5th Battalion Somerset Light Infantry. This is massive too. I mean there are hundreds of us. I've never in my life seen so many men in one place at one time.

This must be serious too because all the ranks are coming with us. We've got officers, of which there must be around 20. I now have also learnt how to tell them all apart. They wear different badges on their sleeves you see, and the officers have a crown. Then there are the Staff Sergeants, probably about 10 of them. They have a small crown and below it three stripes on their arms. The sergeants come next and they don't have a crown above their stripes. But there are more of them. I reckon there must be at least 50. Corporals have only two stripes but there are just as many of them as there are sergeants. I've seen several Buglers too. Actually more than several, maybe 6 or so. I'm guessing they are needed to get our attention; you'd need a loud noise to get this lots attention. Then there are us and we are called 'Privates'. Funny name really isn't it? It just hasn't quite got the same ring to its name as the others do. Oh well, it's what it is, or should I say it is what we are!

We haven't got a badge on our sleeve but we do have a nice badge on our collar. Actually that does have a bugle on it. How many of us lot there are, well you don't expect me to tell you that do you? There are just so many of us. There must be hundreds. Actually it may be even thousands. I'm guessing naturally because I don't know.

We marched for ages and ages. Finally reaching a place called Bulford. I was wondering why here and not at Salisbury Plain, but then one of the older chaps said that this was part of the Plain. As the Salisbury Plain is so vast an area, it is divided into many different Camps with their own names. This one had the name of Sling Plantation. Well, I didn't argue with that and was glad to have reached anywhere at all and just stop.

Removing all our 'offensive dirt', in the form of sweat, was our next task. That felt very good indeed. Boy... was I glad to pull off my boots and socks too. My feet needed a good old soaking, but I settled for a rough bit of cloth and water. I think I've got a blister or two.

Mobilization to Devonport

The war has broken out and I haven't even been here a fortnight when we all hear on the ***4th August*** that we have had orders to pack up and we are being moved to *Plymouth*.

To be quite frank with you, these last few weeks, since my arrival in 'camp' have been so hectic I've hardly had time to think, let alone writing anything down. This has been no ordinary camp either.

Imagine life in a camp going about your daily duties when suddenly a huge cloud bursts open and its bedlam, that'll give you some idea of what it was like. There have even been clouds without the 'clouds' if you grasp my meaning. The clouds are of sand and dirt and not clouds in the sky. We've all had our work cut out just keeping everything free of this dirt. Ah hah... that's probably the reason we've all been brought here in the first place. To get us all accustomed to this sort of life. Is this what it's going to be like in the army? All the time? *Blimey*.

When I got word that the actual *real* war has started it made me feel funny. An enormous lump formed in my belly and I felt frightened. I wasn't quite sure if I was going to have to run to the toilet or be sick on the spot! Of course I didn't let on. Everyone was shouting and raving about like they'd won some prize or something. Why all the commotion? Come on lads, get a grip, it's going to actually come down to fighting and guns and machine guns and all the rest of it. A.J. slapped me on the back and asked me what the matter was. That I should cheer up and join in the bedlam. Cheer up? What the devil is he talking about? It's like this lot really want to fight and use their bayonets and guns.

We also saw what must have been hundreds of new recruits arriving as we were leaving the Plain.

Our battalion were immediately uplifted from camp, 'mobilized' I mean, because that's the word used in the army. We all had to board a train at Salisbury and are headed for Plymouth.

The Station wasn't just around the corner though, we had to march to it. Luckily my blisters had all gone by now and I knew roughly what to expect. In fact I liked this march better and not just because it wasn't going to be as far, but because of the scenery along the way. It still took us about seven hours or so though.

We had to wait for the next train which meant a day later. On ***5th August*** we board the train and our destination is Devonport, Plymouth.

I have never travelled so far in a train before and I found it very long and tiring. I took in all the scenery on the journey though. I didn't want to miss that. Imagine, being able to travel such long distances in trains. I shall certainly tell Dad about me being in this train. Whilst travelling on the train I could also reflect, from time to time in between falling asleep, on my last week's experiences. I did feel a lot fitter after being in 'camp', as time spent there was all about fitness and exercise. Whether I was ready for war though, well that was a different matter. Would any of us ever be ready? Some of the chaps certainly looked the part and couldn't wait, but me, Bill; I don't reckon I am yet.

After reaching Devonport we were split into groups. Our group were to defend the Saltash Bridge which looked so grand I could see why it needed to be protected. Besides the practical side of it that is. I stayed here a few days, then the group I was in marched to another location, which happened to be a primary school called Laira, where we were to be based for several more days. Our duties (wow, saying that makes me feel a soldier already) were to defend the Long Bridge and also the railway. Machine guns were put on both places for the defence.

I felt quite proud to be taking part in this. It was, after all, our first actual 'real' duty at the beginning of this war, and it happened to be bridges which included protecting the trains. My dad will think good of this.

I had a very good time here and was sorry to have to leave.

We were leaving from Devonport but this time there weren't so many of us. We had been split in half, the battalion I mean, we didn't all get on the same train. It was during the night too or should I say early hours of the morning.

It is the ***9th August*** and the train has reached Salisbury. It is still only very early in the morning and we start out on our march towards Durrington Camp, our new destination. Because it had rained intensely the night before we are all still wet, even our rucksacks seem twice the weight. This is going to be a long and tiring march.

Durrington Camp was further too than the previous camp.

Have I mentioned how close we were to Stonehenge? We were really quite close to it, in fact we must have marched passed it many times these last few months. It dates back hundreds of years and is apparently a very sacred place. It is basically a formation of very large stones that form a big circle. Anyhow it is a magnificent sight to see on any day.

Return to Salisbury Plain

Our extensive training for War Service was now officially to take off, with immediate effect. And there I was thinking we'd already been doing extensive training, but apparently we'd only just 'scratched the surface'.

The Plain is perfect for training as its landscape varies enormously. Some parts used to be some sort of burial ground many centuries ago or so the rumours go. Now there's a gruesome thought.

The military camp is also like no other, as here there are many barracks with parade grounds, rifle ranges, and an army hospital and would you believe that there is also a military cinema here! The army have really thought of everything. They are surely doing a wonderful job of looking after us all. Well, I suppose you would have to given that there are literally thousands of men here.

We even get post delivered and I have a letter from Mum and Dad, wishing me good luck with my training and congratulations for turning 17 years old! Blimey, I thought, this is the first time my birthday has come and gone and I hadn't given it a second thought. On ***18th August*** I had become one year older you see. Well what do you know? I knew something was different about me and now I know what it was: I'm a year older already. Mum thanked me also for the postcard I had sent a while back. I haven't mentioned this before but we had had the chance to have our photographs taken to send back to family and friends and it was all done proper, with a special background behind us and all. Mum says Dad has propped it up on top of the shelf in the front room, giving it pride of place.

We had camped here for what must have been at least six weeks, before being moved on ***17th September*** to West down South camp. This camp is still on the vast Salisbury Plain and as I was moving to our new destination I caught a glimpse of the many rows of pointed tents in each area. I can't begin to describe the picture I am seeing. The only way to describe it really is to think of huge settlements with tents in rows and rows.

Have I mentioned the rain? It seems to rain a lot, although it is still summer.

And where there's rain there's mud, and lots of it. I guess with so many pairs of feet marching about the grounds, there would be wouldn't there? I have seen the sense in the putties now though, as without strapping this around our lower limbs our legs would be the worse for wear. It has gotten so muddy inside our tents that we've hung our boots up as high as we can to keep them dry.

They keep on coming too. The men, I mean. More and more arrive on a regular basis. The men come from all parts of the country and many are here all the way from Canada.

I think I am becoming quite a dab hand at the rifle. My shooting skills have much improved whilst I've been here. Well, that'll come in very handy if and when I have to put my skills to the test at battle. What am I saying, putting my skills to the test? I don't think I should be thinking like this at all. It will not be like shooting at a pheasant or a rabbit, will it? Stop it Bill, take a step backwards.

The truth of the matter is we've all been talking about the war and are all worked up and eager to go.

There is talk of us *not* being sent to France, but that we were destined for *India*. Imagine the disappointment many felt when we all got to hear about this. A lot of us lads have had enough now of all the training and want to get 'some real action' in, as we bravely put it.

Despite not yet being able to go to France, men were immediately asked to volunteer for Foreign Services overseas and most of us put up our hands hoping to be chosen. Typically there were far more volunteers than were actually needed, so again a lot of us were very disappointed to find out that we weren't even going to be chosen now.

The Battalion was split up and the 1/4th Battalion left the Camp to prepare for their journey out to India which was going to set sail around the 9th October. I was not among these men.

The rest of us were, however, put back into shape by the end of September and our spirits reignited by a very enthusiastic man with a rather nice name. I heard it once and knew that the name would stick in my memory for a long while to come, it is just one of those names; this man was Lieutenant-Colonel H. F. Clutterbuck. He took command of us all and the 2/4 Battalion was formed.

Word spread around that we were to leave our West Down Camp. On ***5th October*** we were to move back to billets in Bath. I had no idea where 'billets' was, but it turned out to be temporary living space for all of us before our next move. Well I can't help it if I am not familiar with all these new names the army has for things. I certainly am learning though.

Sure enough on ***12th October*** we get to move into Prior Park in Bath, and our new barracks for the time being. This was better. There in the opening of the hedges as I get closer along this lane, I look out onto a very pleasing picture. There ahead of me I see the most magnificent building I have ever seen before in my entire life. I have to stop and take it all in, which almost creates a man pile-up, even though most of the other chaps walk on. 'Could this be the place where we will be staying?' I think to myself, but hadn't *thought* this at all, but had said it out loud, because the lad next to me said he reckoned it surely was. He was as much perplexed as I was. Well, come on describe it to me, you're thinking aren't you? I will say that it's like a massive big stately home. A mansion, you could call it too, with pillars at its front entrance. Proper posh it looked and not what you'd quite expect an army to accommodate.

This was a much nicer place to be marching up to I can tell you.

Colonel Clutterbuck did a real good job here of getting us all back into fine spirits, so to speak. The stamina and vigour was brought back and our frames of mind improved, after not being able to fight just yet.

I VOLUNTEER TO GO TO INDIA

BY ABOUT THE MIDDLE of November more men had arrived and a man, or pardon me but I should say, a General with the name Carew, came on ***27th November*** to inspect the battalion and he explained to us that there might be a possibility we all might very well be needed in India. He was pleased with what Colonel Clutterbuck had achieved with the newly formed battalion. Well, of course we were all very pleased as well with this bit of news. I say we were all very pleased, but there were many among us that had wished they had heard other news; like we'd be off to France or Belgium, not that I really minded. In fact, later that evening me and A.J. decided, if this was to be our destiny and we'd still be doing 'our bit' for the war, then, it's all good news really isn't it?

There followed more lessons including one about malaria fevers. These were told with particular importance and to be taken and noted down very seriously indeed. Now, being a country lad, I have been bitten by mosquitoes many times, but in India they were dangerous. If the mosquito was infected and bit you, it would cause a terrible fever. We were lectured on remembering to keep our hands and feet under the bed sheets at night, as this is when a mosquito bites. If possible to try and get a mosquito curtain if the opportunity arrives. (How this would work around each bed was beyond me). Best to work that one out if and when we get there, I thought to myself.

Then we were explained that a mosquito will lay its eggs in any still water that's lying around. That sounds horrible. Before each night it would be up to anyone of us in our barrack to empty anything which would hold water. Even a fire bucket would have to be checked out.

Enteric fever was another sickness we were all told about. That it is caused through dust in the air. If it fell onto our food and drank we could swallow it. Well this could easily happen when you think about it. The matter of cleanliness was underlined again at this point. We were also advised to eat plenty of fruit and vegetables and not too much meat and bread, as this could cause constipation. Here I am thinking, at home I would have no trouble at this point as we were grown up on fruit and veg.

Another interesting point that was made to us was to protect our body from getting cold. We should especially protect the stomach. We were told that in hot countries people worry too much about the heat and tend to forget the cold. At night the temperature can drop and we were to be sure and wear a flannel belt at night. A flannel shirt should always be worn and to change it as soon as possible if it got wet.

It's ***28th November*** and Colonel Clutterbuck announces that the battalion, as it had now over a thousand men strong, were getting a second chance and we were due to sail for *India* by the end of the year. He told us that the British and Indian Empire had to protect the oil refineries in a place called Abadan, against invasion between the Ottoman and German Empires, that we should take this duty very seriously indeed and our first priorities were to replace regular units that are already in conflict with the Ottoman Empire.

Colonel Clutterbuck explained that men like him, had even before the war began, accepted the obligation of Imperial Service, and he was now asking us to do the same. He wanted us to 'volunteer' ourselves up for service in India.

This is it; we *are* going to go to *India*. This is what we've been waiting for... final confirmation of General Carew's words.

I wasn't even sure where India was but I knew it was some place far away and I'd never ever otherwise get to go there. Of course, we were shown a general map of where India was. I shall now tell you that it is at least half way around the world!

I shall think of it as an adventure. Off to a faraway place.

Yes, I'm going to India.

The men amongst us who still felt let down about not going to *France* to fight were assured that we would most definitely be getting our full share of field service, even in India, before peace would be signed. Also if any man did not want to go to India, they were not obligated to do so and could step out of the battalion if they so wished (I am not sure if anyone did).

Well, I didn't worry one way or the other. I know I've joined the army, but it wasn't really about being real eager to kill or fight somebody. I mean, well, I guess when I joined I wanted to do my bit for King and country, but the thought hadn't entered my mind right then and there that I wanted to go and shoot the enemy. I know that that's what a war is all about, but I still wasn't disappointed about not killing anyone. Any case from what Colonel

Clutterbuck has told us, we'll be fighting the enemy there too. Oh, I don't know, the more I think about it, the more I am confused with my own thoughts on the whole *war* issue. The way I see it, whatever the outcome, the overall experience will be so much more than I could ever have dreamt of.

Never mind Bath or the United States of America - no sirrie - India is the place I'm off too. I will get "broad shoulders" now Dad, you can bet your life on that!

You see my dad always reckoned that if a fellow began to talk cocky about going off somewhere or doing something no-one else would be doing, you would be getting very "broad shoulders"! So that's what I've got now and I like it!

A FIVE DAY LEAVE TO SAY "GOODBYE" TO FAMILY AND FRIENDS

WE WERE GIVEN A five day leave to do with as we pleased and that this would be a good opportunity to go visit family and say our goodbyes. To have to go back home and say 'our goodbyes', blimey did that bring a *knot* into my stomach because for how long would we be gone. These last four months have been the longest I've ever been away from my family. Who knows how long I'll be gone this time? That's why the *knot*. None of us chaps have said anything at all about being away from our families. I did feel it in the beginning. But I had *time* to think more then. When we moved to Salisbury Plain the *thinking* seemed to get less and less. There wasn't time to think. At night I was just to worn out to think, but now.

I had no doubt in my mind what to do with my leave and A.J. said that he intended to do the same. Yes, as it happened we had still somehow managed to stick together, which was great. We had become pals along our journey in training and that felt good. As I might have mentioned before, I was quite a quiet lad and kept somewhat to myself, but me and A.J. seemed to 'click'. We had similar views and shared opinions that other lads didn't.

I'm going to go straight to the Green Park station and hop on a train to Evercreech and let Mum and Dad know about the Battalion I'm in and my journey to India.

On the train back towards Evercreech I'm very excited and I hope that Mum and Dad both don't mind too much about me going so far away. I'm sure they won't mind it too much, especially if I say that I reckon most of the fighting will be in France anyways. I am so busy thinking about what I shall be seeing in India that I almost forget to get out in Evercreech! Don't know where the time just went, but the journey sure was a quick one. I feel much older already. I'm 17 years old and I am off to India.

As soon as my feet step inside our front door, Mum is all over me. The first thing Mum says is "let's ave a look at you son. Are you a being looked after Bill? Are they feeding you plenty? You look tired Bill. How are ya lad? Come. Sit down now. I'll make you a good cuppa tea son and you can tell me all about it."

Where do I start?

Mum wonders if there is a war on over there in 'that there India" (as she put it) too. I say, we're probably going to make sure one doesn't start over there, is what I said. I told her about the oil refineries that we were to go and protect.

Actually, when I got to talking to Mum and Dad, he joined us not long after, I realised I had remembered more than I'd thought I would.

As Mum was so concerned about my well-being, I told her about our lectures in cleanliness and hygiene. Well, that made her eyebrows rouse quite a bit I can tell you but it did the trick and put her mind at rest. I even had the pocket book with me to show her. Dad said that Mum ought to think of my training for the army as much like being at school, but then with more gymnastics!

Dad spoke to me later that evening. Tom and Jesse had been called up for duty on the 5th August. Dad was worried for all of us, he said.

Mum and Dad were very sad to see me go again and my brother Cecil was too. I had a chance now to feel like an older brother when I said goodbye to him, but I guess at least Dad seemed glad he still had a son at home with him. He said he was letting him take over a lot of the chores I used to do for Mum and that it was good for him to grow up all of a sudden. He said he reckoned he did see me grow older all of a sudden.

I must admit though I did feel good in my army uniform and real smart too, that's mums words, but it *did* make me feel good and smart. Of course I had my uniform cleaned up smart enough for the visit and I had given my boots a good old shine before setting off.

Mum shoved a notebook in my hand before I left and she had insisted I write down addresses of family members for sending letters and cards and such and that I should try and keep in touch if and when I could. I would never have thought of that. So I sat right down and wrote out a couple of addresses that Mum read out to me.

Dad left the room then and later walked back in with what looked like a black box in his hands. It was a photo camera. He suggested I take it and if I had the time and opportunity to take a few snap shots, that I should do just that. What a brilliant idea. Anything I saw, Mum and Dad would later be able to see it too, wouldn't they. He gave me some tips on how to work the camera and, he said, most important; don't move when I press the shutter!

It's a clever little box, when you think about it, getting a picture into a box and later being able to look at it on paper. The most amazing part of the camera was, after pressing a little button, how the front part of it suddenly lurches forward like it's on a spring or something. Wow, I never knew Dad had such a precious camera. To be honest with you I don't reckon Mum quite knew either, it was just the look on her face when he produced it that got me thinking this, I could be mistaken though. Unless she was still in shock because of Dad buying it as it looks pretty expensive to me. Perhaps he had opened up his tin box and used some of his small fortune he'd shown us all once; yep I reckon that's what he'd done.

I was quite excited about this camera anyhow and promised Dad I would take very good care of it and carry it at all times with me in my rucksack. Then Dad pointed out that if I needed to use it, I could fit it into my breast pocket! Well, I looked at it again and tried it out for size and, what do you know; it actually did fit inside my pocket. Can you believe that?

I did, however, point out to them both that this was the *army* I was in and that I wasn't going to be there for the pleasure but for services of action. I was trying to take a more serious side here and sound important, that I would have a job to do over there and might not have the time. Dad was quick enough to point out that in times of war they also have photographers too and that I was just to be one step ahead of them in having the chance to grab the image and bring it back home, providing I didn't put myself in any danger of course, providing that. He meant for me to use it during my times off duty and "I was to mind I remember that and not be getting up to no good we it". I made it very clear that I understood exactly what he meant.

Mum and Dad were so sorry and sad to see me off and being December Mum was thinking of Christmas and that I wouldn't be with them. This made matters much worse, but I held back tears and tried to keep a stiff upper lip, like you do, being a young man and all that. It didn't work though. Hey I might be growing older by the minute but I am still human and have feelings. I cried. There, I admit to it. This was the first time I *would* be away so long from my family and it felt strange. I had a knot that was getting bigger in my stomach.

A stranger I sat opposite to on the train journey back to Bath said to me, "well lad, don't you ever be ashamed to have a tear now and then. You just let it out and never give it a thought what anyone else thinks. Well they'll probably go ahead and cry anyway too. No lad it's alright to let your feelings show and don't you let anyone tell you otherwise."

I told him "thank you, sir. I will remember that whenever I feel the urge coming on."

I was so glad to have had time to return to Evercreech and see my family again. I know I haven't been gone that long, but it has felt like I'd been gone ages. Now I am off to another country altogether and another climate altogether too. Am I going to cope alright with the heat? I do like the warmer weather but in India it could be far hotter than I've ever known it here.

I have enjoyed Mum's cooking too and she has spoiled me with her yummy puddings. Mum makes a great bread pudding.

I shall miss that too. Last night she had made my favourite supper, stew with doughboys. (Doughboys are dumplings). I remember Mum saying that she wanted me to get some warm and fattening food into my stomach to last me a day or too, just in case I didn't get a decent meal on my journey. Well, that's typical of any mum now isn't it?

I watch out the window of the 'slow and dirty' and take in the countryside. I watch and enjoy. Who knows how many months it will be before I'm back here again?

12TH DECEMBER 1914: DEPARTURE FROM BATH

WHEN I GET BACK to the barracks in Prior Park, Bath we all have to get prepared and ready for our trip to India. This meant that there was an awful lot of packing to be done.

Colonel Clutterbuck made a speech in the evening instead of giving us an inspection, as it was getting dark and then we all had a good meal. The Colonel said we should tuck in and enjoy as it might be one of our last before our big voyage. Those words had a familiar ring to them.

I showed A.J. my 'pocket' camera after we had eaten. He was very impressed with it indeed and said it was the latest make too; but he also suggested that I had better check with the Colonel and ask his permission to take it with me.

I kind of had an idea that he was going to say that somehow and I spent the next hour worrying myself sick about this camera and trying to pluck up enough courage to go in search of Colonel Clutterbuck.

I didn't manage to locate him but asked a Sergeant instead. My heart was pounding 'ninety-to-the-dozen' and I felt as nervous as hell. God, Bill, pull yourself together, I said quietly to myself.

Well, he came walking towards me and said "what's up lad, what can I help you with?" So I hesitantly showed him the camera and requested his permission that I might take it along with me to India. He took it from my hand and walked away, saying he would check it out for me. My first thought was, oh Christ, he is going to confiscate it right there and then and that was probably the last I'd catch eyes on it. I was pacing up and down that floor so much, I was sure I was going to wear a hole in it. My palms felt sweaty and I wondered if I'd done the right thing.

I could see him approaching in the distance and I had already made my mind up that it was a positive no; when he said "in any other circumstance, I wouldn't be allowed to have it on me, but that as we were off to India, he would allow it".

But that I should only use it, under my own discretion, and to be careful not to upset anyone in the process of doing so. I assured him that I would use it with caution and probably would forget I had it with me anyway. He laughed at this remark and told me not to fret so and that I would probably have many a time to spare to use the camera and if that time should come, not to hesitate in taking the opportunity of doing so. Just before he left me, he turned around and said; "think of it like this lad, will you ever get this chance again?"

In the early hours of 12th ***December,*** I march out of this ancient city of Bath, after hardly any sleep the night before, with a strange feeling inside my belly. A mixture of excitement and anticipation of what lies ahead. A thrill rushes through my whole body making me shiver. The crisp morning, (or night is it actually) doesn't help the shivering and makes it worse.

The sound of the regimental march, played by our battalions' band, is ringing out as we head towards the railway station. The tune seems to echo and pass through each of us as we stamp our shiny boots down onto the tarmac to the rhythms. It is very true that you feel yourself marching with more vigour and ease to bugle music or song. I think back on the first time I learnt to march, to all of us learning to march. It is more difficult than you can imagine, keeping pace together. Putting your left foot forward first and then it's a steady left, right, left, right. Of course this has to be done in perfect timing. My hand and feet coordination was appalling to say the least. The more I concentrated on which foot to put first, the worse I got! Now, today, I don't even really think about it too much.

Right now, at this moment in time, it really did feel *special.*

By the time we reached the station we noticed a small crowd had gathered to give us a farewell. There were so many of us that we needed two trains to take us. The ones that were lucky enough got to step straight into the train standing ready, whereas the not so lucky ones had to wait another hour for the second train to arrive. Yes, you've guessed it; I was among the not so lucky. But the band kept playing to keep up spirits.

When you find yourself hanging around for an hour, that hour seems like a whole day. Was I glad to see that second train come steaming up towards us and stop at the station. I was even gladder to get into it and have a seat, I can tell you!

Songs were sung along the way: "It's a Long Way to Tipperary" and "Pack up your Troubles in your Old Kit Bag". I must have started to doze because I can't remember that entire one. I did join in with "Midsummer Fair" as I know that one very well, but then I fell asleep again.

It was getting late when we finally arrived at Southampton Docks and disembarked the train. We marched right into a scene of ordered chaos! You wouldn't believe what I saw. There wasn't just the one ship (well, I didn't know what to expect) but five of them alongside each other. And, they were all being loaded at the same time! (I realised after, that some were transport ships that were also leaving today).

I saw heavy horses and mules being loaded onto a ship; there must have been at least fifty of them. They were needed for the ammunition carts and water carts and not forgetting machine-gun carts too. I couldn't help but feel sorry for the horses and mules though. They were showing signs of fright even before getting near any action which, mind you, I was hoping they would not have to witness at all.

Other Battalion equipment, of which I heaved a sigh of relief when I heard that we didn't actually have to carry personally, included such items as shovels (there must have been hundreds of them, nearly as many pickaxes, felling axes and hand axes. "Why on earth would an army want so many different axes", I asked A.J. With which he replied, "Well, I suppose we must be going into jungle country and probably will have to fight our way through paths of thick trees or something", I'm guessing though. Another lad said didn't you have to learn how to dig trenches during training? We looked at each other. Ooh, that explains the shovels and axes. I saw machine guns too.

But we had other things on our minds. We were being drilled and marched and drilled again and, well quite frankly, we were by now getting all fused up so to speak.

A chap next to me, well boy, he was so fused up you could have lit a match right there and then and I reckon he would of shot off to India of his own accord!

We certainly were all raring to go.

Departure from Southampton on the S.S. Saturnia

When I got a good look at this ship I was about to set foot on, it almost took my breath away. Now I don't know much about ships and I can't say I've ever set foot on one, because I haven't, but this one looked huge. It had big steam funnels and lots of small windows and tall masts. It made me feel very small. I got a funny feeling in my stomach, I can tell you.

Its name was the S.S *Saturnia*. With a name like that it sounded just like it could have come straight out of one of my annual adventure books that I used to read when I was younger. I could be about to have a secret journey, stepping into a real life story. So what if I am a bit of a romantic? There is no harm in that is there?

When I walked up that boarding plank I stopped for just a moment, took a deep breath, looked at the buzz of activity below us, and stepped on board. There is no going back now. I'd look like a complete 'nutter' if I decided to take off and run back down. That knot is back inside my belly though.

The ship sets sail – slowly and gently it leaves the Port. We were off.

I shall never forget this moment ever. The excitement and the sight around us was a feeling you could only imagine if you had been there. Other ships were setting off alongside us. These were the ships with the horses and the ammunition and all the rest of the equipment that was needed to be transported for us.

When I got below deck (which I'd preferred later rather than sooner), the scenery was a whole different 'kettle of fish' if you'd excuse my expression. The only way to describe the scene was to imagine bodies of all shapes and sizes waving their arms and feet about and passing rucksacks to one another.

The quarters were cramped and hot and stuffy. I didn't feel too special for about a week. But I was not the only one by far. There weren't many with "sea-legs" as they called them. If you could get up on the deck you felt much better though. Although it was very cold the air was fresh and the wind helped blow away the sick feeling and the stuffiness of our quarters. It felt real good to breath in the sea air. I had had more than my share of farm air during my lifetime, but this was even greater in comparison. The air felt different, and smelt good and fresh. Not like being at the seaside either. Just think; I said to myself, Bill, you are now travelling on the Atlantic Ocean, who would have thought.

It didn't help much having to sleep in a hammock either! I tried to get on deck as much as possible. After a week went by I finally got settled down to being on the sea. We were left pretty much alone too. No drilling, not that there would have been room to drill anyhow, by the way.

The whole ship was crammed full, what with the blokes and bags of equipment.

Also we weren't the only Battalion on board, as we discovered there were also blokes from Wiltshire and Devon.

I kept hold of my greatcoat and blanket too and carried them with me on deck. Not that the uniform was thick enough, because it was rather, but if I felt dozy I needed the extra warmth of the coat and blanket and was able to stick it outside for a lot longer than other chaps from my group.

After a while I also preferred sleeping on the floor to sleeping in the hammock. A little less motion!

I didn't eat much the first week either. Felt too seasick to eat. Everybody was seasick. One of the Corporals from my group who was assigned to keep an eye on us younger lads, did coax me into drinking hot soup though with a crust of bread, after a lot of tempting mind you, as like he said, "you've got to get something warm inside you lad".

If I could sneak into the kitchen and grab a hot bun, I would mind you. You could just about crawl between cupboards now and then to get hold of one. I'd shove it into my trouser pocket and get out as quick as I could so no-one would notice.

You might well be thinking ah hah, Bill is getting up to no good and you would be correct to think such a thing. It's what I did do. Well, what else was there to do on board a huge ship in the middle of the ocean on my way to some big adventure?

Wow, guess what I have just witnessed? I've come on deck for some more fresh air and as I lean against the side of the ship, I look up and see an amazing sight. *Flying fish!* Well, okay, they haven't got wings or anything like that. I may have just exaggerated a tiny bit. But hey, I haven't set eyes on anything like this before. The fish seem to literally jump out of the water, make an arch, and dive back in the water again. I just had to share this with you.

Porridge or a sort thereof was another of my favourites. I would get that down pretty quick I can tell you, especially if it was nice and creamy. It didn't taste as good as mums porridge though, as we were lucky if we tasted any sugar in it.

I slept a lot on the journey. I figured I'd get enough sleep as I could because there was talk that we'd be marching in India at night a lot, being as it was so hot there. I can't imagine it being hot if I'm so cold right now. But sleep was best I thought. If I slept I didn't feel the ship going up and down with the big waves and all. Oh, and by the way there were a heck of a lot of huge waves and gusts of wind. Chaps were still being ill all over the place.

It was when we were reaching Cape Finnesterre that the Colonel decided to get us all up on the deck for some fresh air. The sea had gotten calmer and well quite frankly it was necessary to get the quarters cleaned up after all our mess.

Anyhow it was good to set eyes on some land too as we passed the Cape of St. Vincent. We did a bit of drilling and parading for want of some needed exercise.

The sun was shining too and I perked up a bit, feeling less sick.

By the way, these place names I've been telling you about, you've probably been wondering how I know them, but you see I have been looking at a map and listening to fellow soldiers talking as I've been walking on deck. Not only that but it's nice to be able to say to someone later on in my life that I have been or passed by there.

If there wasn't much else to do on the ship I found myself day-dreaming too. Mostly I would start thinking of Mum and Dad back home. Not trying too much, as I do admit I'd get rather homesick if I did that, so tried *not* to do that too much. Best not too. No-one would get far feeling homesick and all.

When I heard blokes talking about the Gibraltar Straights and that we were now going to be travelling through it and passing Africa, it got me all excited and I thought it can't be too long now and we'll be able to get off this ship.

The next day when I stepped on deck the sun was shining quite bright and we were sailing passed the coast of Portugal.

Hitting a Banana Boat!

It's an early Friday morning on ***18th December*** and we reach Gibraltar. I have reason to jot this date down as will come clear shortly. Here I am on deck having a good time and looking at the cliffs and feeling excited at the ruggedness of the land, and not only the land on the left of us but also on the right of us. I could see both sides of this part of the sea. On the Spanish side I caught a glimpse of snow on the highest peaks of the mountains. It is a narrow strip of sea, where (I heard this later on) the Atlantic stops and the Mediterranean begins.

Suddenly I hear shouts, followed by a thump which jolted us, then this strange scraping noise. There seemed to be quite a commotion on board and more shouting's were heard. We had run into a banana boat, if you've ever heard of such a thing! I'm only quoting what someone else said it was. Of course, when I managed to get a good look, it was a fishing schooner. Didn't resemble a banana at all. Why the devil would anyone call it that? I don't know. Boats also apparently can have nicknames!

Oh don't worry, there were no casualties. Our ship had to stop though to find out what damage was done to the boat.

It delayed us by a day and it also separated us from the transport ships that were accompanying us. They were out of sight. I guess they didn't bother to hang around and wait for us, but carried on their way. I got the idea that this was not taken too kindly by the higher ranks as it left us alone and vulnerable.

Oh wow. I am on deck again enjoying the freshness of the air and making the most of the sun, when I look down along the side of the ship and catch sight of something. There are these sharks in the water and they just look as though they are doing their best to keep up with the ship. I give A.J. a shout to come and take a look. Well, when he takes a look, he calls out to one of the sergeants to take a look too. He guesses that they are probably bottlenose sharks. Well, before long lots more soldiers come to take a look. What a sight this was. They do look very strange to me. Almost as if they have something that shouldn't be there, stuck on their noses; most peculiar. This is turning out to be a real adventure, witnessing all these wonderful sights.

We are on the Mediterranean Sea now and the weather is nice and warm. The sea is so gentle – not even a ripple. A very pleasant feeling I can tell you, after all the turmoil of the rough and absolutely awful North Sea and Atlantic Ocean. Oh, I can't even bear thinking of it now. I think now we've all started to recover a bit and come on deck, they're glad down below to be able to give it a much needed clean up! I pity the poor fellows doing that job, bah!

Let me quickly change the subject.

We've had our Sunday service, despite not having any vicar to do the job, that didn't seem to hold matters back as our Colonel stepped in. Of course he ended with giving us a bit of a briefing on India while he was at it.

I took the chance after our service to write a small note to Mum and Dad, wishing them a Happy Christmas and letting them know that I was doing alright. I didn't let on that I'd been so sea-sick and of the state of the ship. That would have been too much information I reckon. Best not to tell too many details or they'll already wish they hadn't consented on letting go of me.

I don't know when they will come around and collect the mail from us but I'm sure they will as soon as we stop alongside some place.

Have I mentioned the sunsets I see from the ship? Flipping fantastic is what I'd say to that. It really takes my breath away. The sun just seems to melt away in the background. It's scenes like this that you kind of think, well if the worse were to happen; at least these will be among my memories and will stay with me forever. No-one can take this away. The sea is also so amazing. Sometimes it is so calm and as smooth as can be. The only movement being the waves or shall I say ripples that our ship makes and yet if the weather changes, so does the sea.

We'd been told back at Southampton that we'd be landing at Port Said, Egypt.

I reckoned it was best to think ahead. Imagine this *India*. How far is India from Egypt that's what I was thinking right then? How many marching days! Or do they have trains there too?

What will it be like I'd wonder to myself?

Suez Canal

When we drew up alongside Port Said we saw a load of other ships nearby. All of these large ships had troops on board that had already seen fighting and were on their way back home. I guess we're one of the ships ready to relieve these troops. New strengthening power as you might say.

There is really a war on here too, it dawned on me. What was I thinking? There couldn't possibly be a war going on here? That *war* hadn't come so far from home? It sure did give me a lump in my throat, I can tell you. And no amount of swallowing seemed to dislodge it either. A saying came immediately to my mind; you know the one, 'calm before the storm'.

We arrive at ***Port Said*** on ***24th December,*** Christmas Eve. Strange, I think, it's warmer than some of our summers, and it's Christmas, which, by the way, I had almost forgotten. It wasn't until I heard some chaps mention it, that I realised. I wonder if we will be allowed off the ship.

We spent Christmas Day at Port Said, which was a good thing as all us lads had to find our "land-legs". If you kept still for too long you felt like you had forgotten to get off the ship! Wait a minute; I am not off the ship yet!

We did get to have our Christmas dinner aboard though and I must say it was the best meal ever. Well, I suppose it would be, not having a proper meal for ages being so seasick and all.

Christmas Day was not so lucky either for some of us chaps. They are calling it the "black day". Why? Because the day was spent coaling! I heard someone mention how they thought that the Egyptian boys were the filthiest they think they'd ever set eyes upon! Well, I've got news for you; we're not going to look much different at the end of the day either!

I took out my notebook that Mum had given me to just jot down a couple of notes. What do you reckon I found inside my notebook? A photograph of my mum. Oh god, I feel a tear starting to form. What a nice thought, but that's mums for you isn't it. Luckily it was small so I decided to push it into one of my breast pockets of my combat uniform so as to be close to me at all times. What can I say? I am just a lad with feelings. So, get over it.

Other blokes had photos of their 'sweethearts' close to them. Well, I haven't got one of them yet.

Boxing Day is a quiet day for us. Sergeants were allowed off the ship and got to look around. None of us really minded though. We were still tired from coaling. I still wasn't completely rid of the black stuff. I'd felt cleaner on the Plains than I did right now. But then again, this was an adventure and you don't go on an adventure without getting dirty, do you?

It's Sunday ***27th December*** and after the ship had taken on a new supply of coal we were on our way again sailing down through the ***Suez Canal***. I can't believe I've even just said that, who would have thought that I would be doing this a month ago?

It's a lot narrower than I had imagined it to be. You might think to yourself, isn't a canal a narrow strip of water, but I hadn't been thinking along those lines. We were, after all, travelling between two countries.

There is an atmosphere on board of suspension as we are so close to both Egyptian and Arabian land that we are almost afraid if the Turks might be hiding in waiting.

We soon stop worrying though when we see a Camp of the 'Camel Corps', as I heard they were called.

Apparently the Canal is guarded on the eastern banks by Indian troops against attack from the Turks.

I'll tell you how near we are; we can hear the Indian troops wishing us all the best of luck and cheering away, which give us all a bit of a boost.

In fact a band belonging to the Wiltshire Battalion appears out of nowhere on deck, and starts playing a tune. A gunboat carrying French soldiers passes us during our journey down and when the band stop playing, the troops on board the gunboat start cheering out loud. We all cheer back. What a day!

After the lonely journey along the Mediterranean this was something else. There was something interesting to see all the time.

We even have to pull alongside at one stage to let another ship pass! Now that'll give you an idea of how wide the canal is.

We stop at ***Suez*** in the evening, but it was only for a short while. Apparently we are changing captains! When I hear about this I think to myself, I don't blame the captain either; he deserves a rest after piloting us down this far.

We leave the narrow Suez Canal behind us and now travel down the ***Gulf of Suez***. I can still see the land though and it looks quite rough and high in places. We have left the canal behind us and the sea is getting wider now.

Before long we are heading down the ***Red Sea*** and into a much wider stretch of water.

It was very hot in our quarters. Reel stuffy. You had trouble to fall asleep it was so stuffy. I guess these extreme conditions are to be expected now.

First we had grumbled at being sea-sick and now we're all grumbling because it's too hot to stick lying in our hammocks!

Not to mention the after effects of our inoculations which, by the way, I'd forgotten to mention. These were given to us by the doctor on board. It was not an item to be refused. We all had to have these 'jabs' for our "own well-being"(as we were reminded). "After all", the doc said, "you are all heading for strange territory and a different climate, and no doubt different food and drink. You all need a little help with this sudden change and that's what this injection is for."

It was to be the first of many.

When I stand on deck and look at the distant landscape, I can just about see the rugged mountains and it gets me thinking of what lies beyond them. I mentioned earlier on about the things I have read in the schoolboy annuals and can't help but pinch myself literally in the flesh. Why? Don't you understand what I'm getting at? This journey I am making will be like jumping into one of my books to me. I am looking out from this ship and way beyond the land ahead lays deserts and Arabia. And on the other side of the ship, if I look out far across the land is Egypt. I was even closer to Egypt on the Suez Canal. It has just sunk in that I have been within a small distance of a land that you only read of in the bible.

I know that right now, even as I stand here dreaming away, somewhere else in France there are other chaps actually fighting a war. I realise this, but they are there and I can't help being where

I am now. I could have been sent to France too, but it wasn't to be. I wanted to, but wasn't picked, and instead put my hand up and volunteered for the next best thing and got picked for here, and so did A.J. and other chaps too. I have wondered since this journey if I should have hung around and waited to go to France, but then again how long would the wait have been? We were all of us in that spur of the moment decision-making and after all our training we all of us just wanted to take the chance to do our bit. All I know is I am stood here right now and my mind keeps filling up with all these thoughts and I have no way of changing this. Bill, I say to myself, you can't help it that it's taking us so long to get to wherever it is we have to be... I start to shiver and I decide I've had enough of 'thinking' and fresh air for today. I need to get a grip and mingle amongst the chaps more.

On the 22nd November 1914 the British had already put up a fight against Ottoman soldiers in the city of Basra, Mesopotamia. The Ottoman soldiers retreated after a short fight and made their way further up the river. The British occupied the city and kept order there. At the battle of Qurna, further up the river Tigris the British managed to capture Commander Suphi Bey and 1,000 of his Ottoman troops.

The British were now in a strong position and could ensure that Basra and the oilfields were protected from an Ottoman advance. The main Ottoman army was a further 275 miles north-west around the city of Baghdad.

❖ ❖ ❖

1915

Bombay to Bangalore

In fact, it takes us a whole week to travel the red sea, and on ***New Year's Day, 1st January*** we pass a place called ***Aden***. It must be strange living there too, because it looks as though it is surrounded by very jagged cliffs which seem to cut through the place.

We all notice that now the temperature during the nights will drop right down low and this takes some getting used to. It makes me shiver a lot. We are approaching (we've been told) the last part of our journey and travelling on the ***Arabian Sea***.

It isn't quite so stuffy during the day either, because there seems to be a cool wind blowing across from the ocean. This didn't bother any of us at all. The one thing bothering some of us now seemed to be the after effects of our inoculation! Can't beat it all I suppose. My arm isn't much of a bother. A bit achy and stiff, that's all.

After a while we lose sight of any land and for a further week there is none in sight. We do get to witness a whale shark. Well that's what I heard it was anyway. I was crouched on deck with my eyes shut enjoying the quiet, when suddenly someone nearby lets out such a shout it practically launches me right in the air. So I jump up as quickly as I can and this chap is still shouting for us to look to the starboard side of the ship. It caused such a stir, but got everyone moving to just the one side of the ship. It was a sight worth shouting about though. None of us had ever seen anything like as big as that shark was. Blimey I wouldn't want to swim in these waters, I can tell you. Unfortunately he was quite a way out so I didn't get a close look, but I did notice that it looked darker than normal sharks.

We reach ***Bombay harbour*** on ***8th January*** and I feel so excited about getting here. There wasn't time to stand and admire though as it was all hands on deck. We spend all day unloading the equipment and baggage. By the time night falls we are completely exhausted.

Our stay here was not to be a long one either, as we are told that same evening that we are leaving for a place called ***Bangalore***.

I've just realised I am standing for the first time on Indian soil!

A very long train awaits us for the next part of our journey and by the time we all get into the train it is gone midnight. We all get under our blankets to keep us warm and are given a drink of tea, which is cold!

I was quite excited when I heard that we were to be travelling nearly one hundred miles on a train through India, but now that I realise it's going to be all through the night, I'm not so sure. I won't see anything at all. Not that I mind first of all, because no sooner than we are off, I keep falling in and out of sleep! But it would have been interesting to take a *look* at the scenery while travelling such a way. Not that I can get to a window to look mind you. We are so crammed into this wagon it's almost impossible to move; it makes me think of the phrase, packed like 'sardines in a tin', as that'll give you an idea of how it is. I wake up loads of times with the cold and am glad of the blanket. We seem to be climbing at one point through mountains and you can hear the wind making strange whistling and creaking noises between the carriages. It's very different from being on the ship, very eerie too. I fall in and out of sleep for most of the journey in fact and each time when I wake up, I sit up and wonder where the hell I am; then I realise and just sit, lean back again and close my eyes. My mind has gone blank....

The journey from *Bombay* to *Bangalore* turns out to be quite an eventful one, if I can even call it that, as it was also, if I'm truthful horrific too. We had to get onto these rather small looking wagons. There were many of these wagons thankfully to carry all of us that were in the Somerset Light Infantry that is, I also remember it being very long. Perhaps I ought to mention that not all soldiers on board the ship got to join us. Some had to go north, which meant we most likely wouldn't see a lot of the chaps we'd spent so many days on board with ever again.

In places the railway track was very steep, as we were travelling through what they called the Western Ghats of India.

At one stage of our journey the train suddenly stopped for no reason at all and we all thought we'd need to get out and push the thing! But this wasn't the case after all.

It was explained that we did, however, have to unload everything we had with us, including all our equipment and load it all back onto another train waiting, which even looked to be a smaller type. Could it get much smaller? I thought to myself. This smaller train would take us the rest of the way.

Thinking about it, it's probably just as well I can't look out a window. My dad always said, "Bill, sometimes it does best not to know everything that happens" and "Bill if you knew everything beforehand you wouldn't do anything at all." "Just take it as it comes to you in life", is what he used to say to me. Well, that certainly applies to me right now. The sounds of the train were enough on its own to give me 'goose-bumps', let alone the cold. By the way, I am now convinced that wind definitely *can* howl!

We finally arrive at ***Bangalore*** on ***12th January****;* it's early in the morning and we clamber out of our confined spaces. My legs nearly quiver as they touch ground and move about. I have to stretch them and the rest of my limbs to wake myself up before looking around. What a journey. But, like another chap said, "you'd better get used to it, because I reckon there'll be a lot more of these to come".

Now we have to load ourselves up for a three-mile march to our new Barracks. That'll stretch the legs and get the blood pumping I guess.

Our march into barracks feels good too as we are literally 'played in' with an escort from a native band. I didn't expect that to happen at all. Well, I don't know what I expected. Although I don't reckon anybody else expected this surprise either. It was a great way to welcome us though.

The barracks are not a lot different from the ones on Salisbury Plain. The only difference being it's not muddy here and feels much warmer!

We spend the rest of the day sorting equipment out and unloading baggage. It feels good to grab the chance later in the afternoon to have a wash and get 'freshened up' after our long and tiring train journey. Afterwards it's just heaven to be able to lie flat and slowly fall into a deep sleep. Although I felt that I'd slept a lot on the train, it was more like a dozing off and a startling awakening, than a proper sleep. It seems everybody is the same and we are left alone for this purpose.

I awaken to loads of chattering and movement inside our barracks. I realize I am half dressed already, which turns out to my advantage when I ask what the hell is going on, only to be told we have to report for 'parade'. Although we are now in India with different surroundings, we are still the Somerset Light Infantry and are here for a mission and that also includes normal duties! I suppose we ought to be thankful for the rest.

I try my best to focus myself, get washed and properly dressed and give my boots a good earned clean and a polish.

It's 7a.m. and we stand and parade. This is followed by our 'physical drill'.

Afterwards we get to check over our equipment and are also told that we can get the chance of a *Puggaree* at the Quarter Master Stores building between 10 and 11 a.m. if we like. A Pug-a-what? It was explained to us that it's a lot like a hat with a wider rim. It could be very useful when the sun gets really hot. I think I'll pass on that one for the moment. I have always been used to the sun. I think I can always cover my head with something and improvise if the time arises.

When I, and the rest of us, get a chance to familiarise ourselves with our new barracks, I get the feeling that the 'British' have really settled here and prepared themselves for this whole situation.

I say this because there is actually a British Soldiers Club, called the Y.M.C.A. Building just down the road from here. I read this from a notice pinned to one of the barrack walls.

I suppose it's all had to be established to work and be very practical for the hundreds of us soldiers who will be around until the war has ended.

The notice reads:

NOTICE

Men can exchange English money at Bank rates for Indian coinage at Y.M.C.A. Buildings, Ulanr Road (British Soldiers Club) from 5-7 every evening.

Rates for exchange are:-

6d.for 5 annas
1/- for 10 annas.
2/- for 1 Rupee 5 annas
2/6- for 1 Rupee 11 annas
10/- Gold for 7 Rupee 8 annas

Men are advised not to go to the Bazaar to change money as they will not get proper rates of exchange.

I Settle in and Use my Camera

The next couple of days are pretty much the same. We are awakened at 7 a.m. for parade and physical drills.

One extra parade at 9.30 a.m. is followed by discussions over our rates of pay and allowances. We are all allowed 2 annas per day for kit allowance. I am going to have to get used to this new money. There's a lot to take in.

Another notice appears:

NOTICE
Hindustani classes for N.C.O's. and Men
are held every day except (Thursdays and Sundays)
in the Regimental School from 4 to 5 p.m.

I have had no time to think of the camera that I've carried with me since we left. Apart from one time on board the ship that I did think about getting it out, but I didn't want to attract any attention to myself. A camera would have attracted attention no doubt and I just wasn't up to it. I probably wouldn't have kept a steady enough hand to take a picture anyhow.

However, when I'd managed to have a moment to myself I decided to slip away and take in my whereabouts. A.J. came with me. Well, as a matter of fact, I didn't quite fancy walking off barracks alone. Call me what you will, I don't care; I just feel safer being with another chap that's all. India seems a strange land.

We decided not to wander too far off.

I kept the camera in my pocket until I came across something different, other than the people. We could see some buildings nearby and thought we'd have a look around them.

As we approached them we noticed shapes in the bricks. I saw not just shapes, but actual animals beautifully formed in the stone. There seemed to be only two animals. But these two were repeated in the stonework. One was of a horse, but the other animal I wasn't too sure about.

"I don't know about you A.J. but I reckon I'm seeing two heads?"

"No," said A.J. laughing, "it has one long neck and head and a very long tail."

"Okay then, if that's a long tail, then why is it stood straight up and not hanging down like it should be?"

"How should I know the answer to that?" said A.J. "Maybe it did that when they carved it."

There were two animals carved in the stonework. One of a horse, the other I wasn't too sure about. It looked as though the animal had two heads!

Camp life: Getting accustomed to the natives.

Well, whatever, it was worth taking a photograph of this wall, is what I thought. We both looked around to see if we were being watched, before I produced the camera. You could never be too careful.

I took the plunge, made the picture and decided I'd leave it at that. I was *not* going to take a photograph of any natives. Well, what if they got offensive? This is a time of war. No, I've taken my first shot, am happy to have recorded this curiosity on its own and leave it at that for now. I put the camera back in my pocket. "Let's get back to our barracks" I said to A.J. I had neither the courage nor confidence to *go looking* any further, although A.J. would have liked to, he agreed to go back.

I must just let you know that although I didn't dare to take a picture of the natives here, it wasn't because I wouldn't have wanted to. The colours I notice they are wearing are just lovely. The women wear pretty bangles on their wrists too which really attract my eyes but I do my best not to stare in case they are offended. Until I know more about the culture and what might be allowed, I think it's best to stay a little bit cautious. Yes, I can be sensible if I put my mind to it; I'm in an army uniform for pity sake so I must, mustn't I?

I have a parcel from Mum to open and inside I find she has sent me some Cadbury's chocolate and some of my favourite bread pudding and a letter. She tells me all sorts of local news including:

> *"Our new Vicar is called Mr. Bonsey and he's doin a proper job. He even is getting in a lorry en goin round the farms collecting the milk. It's bloomin comical to see and he does it on Sundays too afore takin his early service. His wife is doin her bit too as she's in charge of the Red Cross VAD's along wi Mrs. Sherston. They been getting young nurses to help in Shepton Mallet wi a Military Hospital that as been created in a couple of ouses up ther."*

That was just the sort of things I enjoyed reading about in Mum's letters. I can just picture that Vicar with his collar on and his 'wellies' going about his rounds on the farms.

Moving to Calicut

By ***16th January*** we were all beginning to settle down and get accustomed to our new surroundings. We had a *tailor,* who was a local man called Ellai, and he was available to us if any alterations to our kit were needed. He was also the man to see when we heard we would be getting two pairs of Khaki Shorts each. Our first pair was supplied free of charge and the second pair of shorts was for one half the cost of the regiment and the other half would be deducted from our pay. This, when I gave it some thought, was fair enough. Imagine the cost involved in supplying us lot? We were only too pleased to hear that we were all getting supplied with shorts in the first place. I thought at first it was only a luxury for the officers, as some already had been given them on board the ship.

It'll be a relief, during the day, to change into something more wearable to suit the climate here. One bloke did mutter a bit under his breath the words "which half of the shorts are the army going to want back afterwards" though, which made us see the funny side of it.

A *Shoe Maker* with a name ending in ...awmy (don't ask me what the first bit was because I didn't quite catch it) would be available to repair our boots if or when necessary. No doubt with all our marching, he will come in very handy! Although, I wonder if that means he comes along with us when we go on a mission or something. I doubt it very much, but the thought's there.

Another native with an even longer name had his own personnel whom we could use to our discretion. These men were called *dhobis* and would be doing our washing for us. And, wait for it, if we were desperate and needed clothes washed in a hurry, there was even a *'flying dhobi'* too. No, he didn't actually fly, he would get on his ox (or whatever it was) and he'd be off as quick as a flash. Of course, the cost of having our washing done was 14 annas a month (which was deducted from our pay) or you could pay 1 anna an item if you used the quicker method. Blimey I'd pay 1 anna just to see this 'flying dhobi' in action.

Well now, of course, there was also a native *Barber* too with another difficult name to pronounce. I shall have to listen real hard to catch their names next time around. We could have our hair cut for 2 annas a month and as often as we wished. There was no allowing for hair to be cut by any other means but to go to this Barber! In other words no cutting of each other's hair! However for a shave we have to pay 2/4 of an anna for one shave at a time. I did find out later on that it was also possible to buy a book of 32 tickets for a cost of 8 annas, which I think covered the lot, but quite frankly I managed without the book. I didn't have a shave as often as I should have had, but I also wanted to *keep* some money at the end of the month too!

All this extra information was a lot to take in. It's all a lot to take in. I can't get my head around half of it, I can tell you.

I haven't mentioned the food yet, which was rationed somewhat, although we were allowed some extra food to the value of about 2 annas 6 pie a day. Also we had the opportunity of buying fruit off of the natives, who were known as *Fruit Hawkers*. It was pointed out to us that on all these occasions to make sure the Fruit Hawker wore a brass armlet with "S.L.I." on it; otherwise they were not to be trusted. In fact the ones with the armlets were only allowed into the barracks anyway. But the odd figure might slip in, so to be on the alert. See what I mean about a lot to take in? I suppose I'll get the hang of it.

We have a Dress Drill. This gives me a purpose to shine my boots, buttons and belt extra hard. It also includes carrying our rifles. I make sure that it is cleaned and in top condition. Not that I don't keep my rifle cleaned, because I do. But you know how it is when you have that extra reason to make an even better job. A well kept rifle meant that it would stay in top condition in our time of need.

We all parade on what's known as the Barrack square. Here I am then standing proud and ready for just about anything that'll be thrown my way and it's at this moment that I actually begin to *feel* like a soldier. What I mean precisely is that only now, at this stage in my journey, does it begin to register mentally that I am on a duty; and not just me, of course, all of us. But I feel it now more than ever. Holding this rifle. I am possibly going to use it in my defence, and it's very real. This is *not* an adventure. But this could become a definite reality; the question is when and where?

The remainder of today is a casual day but as we are told we will be leaving early tomorrow, we also have to prepare for another train journey.

As its Sunday we all go to a church service. I may not have mentioned before about going to Church. Even though we were in the army there has always been a service on a Sunday. But I start to think about what might happen when I, and the other lads, get to the front line where the action is. There will be no opportunity then to pop off on Sunday to Church will there? Normal life will cease. I find myself praying. I pray for peace of mind. Will *he (God)* be able to forgive me, when I reach that moment and find myself forced to use my rifle?

In the early hours of ***17th January*** I and all of 'B' Company stand ready on Barrack square for our orders to march to Bangalore Station. Some of us are going on from there to Malapuram and some on to Calicut.

I am going with the Company to a place called *Calicut*, and there I was thinking we were in for a long stay at this place. In actual fact our Company has only had four days here which is short, considering Bangalore is a fine place.

We arrive at *Calicut* early Monday morning on ***18th January.*** Although it doesn't look far on a map, it is rough country, believe me, with steep hills and forests. It was another tiring journey on the train. I could kick myself too for dozing off so many times. I had wanted to take in the scenery on the way but I just felt so tired. I reckon it could be the heat making me so weary. Blimey at one stage I felt a bit overwhelmed by it all and this must have shown because I got given a punkah, which is a fan that I could hold in my hand to get some air moving. It's only January but here the temperature is as hot as most English summers.

The days followed with Physical Drills and Recruit Drills. There were several Districts that were strictly out of bounds; the reasons of which were not given.

We are right by the coast here which helps out with the heat a bit.

I will write a letter to Mum and Dad. Yes, that's what I will now do. We have some time-out in the afternoons because of the heat. I will try and put her mind at rest and let her know that I am well and safe and being looked after. I shall explain about the money here and a little of our surroundings.

As the sun gets warmer in the later part of the afternoon, we are allowed to parade in short sleeve shirts. Thank goodness!

My friend A.J. dies

There is going to be a school of Musketry starting on 29th January at a place called Satara. Well, I am going to put my name down for that. I think it best to learn as much as possible.

Have I mentioned that we get biscuits and tea at 6.30 a.m.? From Thursday ***21st January*** it has come into our daily rations. We all get the same. Mind you it costs us 3 pie a day for this little luxury, but hey, we are British you know and a cup of tea without a biscuit is like a scone without the cream. But even though I mention the cost, we do make the most of our tea and really appreciate it. On Sundays we have the tea and biscuits an hour later, at 7.30a.m and after our Church Parade we have our breakfast.

Some soldiers are detailed for particular duties; such as helping with the Dairy Farm, or helping the Regimental Police. Others are detailed to the Gymnasium or the Garrison Military police or even to act as Clerk to the Assistant Director of the Medical Services. I wonder if I will be detailed for anything.

NOTICE
The Mile Race and Mile Bicycle Race
are open to all British Troops.
Men wishing to enter must apply to
the Adjutant on the Ground by 3.30 p.m.

It's Saturday ***23rd January*** and I have just spotted this notice. I think that I am going to have a go at this Race. I can ride a bicycle pretty quick. I wonder if A.J. will be a sport and have a go too.

I didn't win but the ride was fun and pretty invigorating except for coming out in a great old horrible sweat at the finish and had to lie on the ground for some while to get over it.

Several months have passed. I haven't written anything else down as there hasn't been a lot to tell you. I mean it would be rather boring if I just wrote page after page about our daily drills and parades. Each day has gone and passed and I have really settled down now. I have felt the sun get hotter these last few months. We are now into the month of ***April*** and the temperature has peaked even higher. Which I can tell you is yet another hurdle to climb over. I'm sure it's well in to the 90 degrees. We are all in this together though and just have to make do and get on with it. At least we have no trouble washing. Maybe this is why we are here for a while, that's what I am thinking.

We're being allowed to acclimatize and refresh our souls!

Well I am up for this, I can tell you.

Although the temperature is hot it does feel fairly damp as we're only a few miles away from the sea. In fact our Barracks do overlook the sea as we seem to be on a hill.

We cannot get away from the Barracks and go visit anywhere though, which is a bit of a shame.

But I've overheard the Officers talking and there does seem to be other sorts of diseases in this area, so I gather that's why we're not let out of these boundaries that we still have. Also the water available cannot be drunk straight from its source, but has to be boiled first.

But I've realised that after staying here a while it hasn't all been plain sailing. After all, this turns out to be like a tropical rain forest area. More often than not we get quick showers of rain, which means *when it rains it doesn't half blooming rain*! At first too, I would feel a sigh of relief for the rain and want to stand in it and get wet. I tried this a few times, but wouldn't recommend it. No, now I just run as fast as I can and find shelter out of the rain. The air cools down anyway for a short while, which gives some relief.

After the rain the steam will hang around the Barracks in the afternoons and it makes our uniforms feel really unpleasant.

The flies and mosquitoes are a damn nuisance. I am often tempted to leave my shirt off, but this is not an option, unless you want the mosquitoes to come and have a 'field day' with your blood! I've never known so many around one person. It gets annoying and that's putting it mildly. The trick is to not expose your skin too much; otherwise you'd be fresh blood for a mosquito.

Of course, I've noticed A.J however, not taking a bit of blind notice to such advice and he'd, sure enough, get bitten by a mosquito and up would come a swelling of his skin and he'd curse and scratch and scratch and curse.

Some chaps are not at all well. In fact many have already been sent away to somewhere else to get medical attention. It is this disease the mosquitoes bring with them that was talked about. It is happening now. I just can´t believe that it´s only the beginning of April and it´s so bloody *hot!*

My friend and best mate, A.J., is among the chaps who are not well. There is a fever spreading and what with the bad heat, it is just too much to bear for them. I hope he perks up and will get better soon. I am not looking forward to having to miss him if he gets sent home. The doctor is keen to send some who are fit enough to travel, to a place called Wellington. But at the moment A.J isn't fit to even stand on his own two feet so he can't be sent there.

We seem to be doing so much drilling and most of this is from very early in the morning until the afternoon. Then we have to stop because it's too hot, so we get a rest.

That gives me a chance to nip over to the sick bay and take a sneak at A.J. He's not doing well at all. Please don't leave me A.J. Don't die on me. I realize he *could* die.

I've not had much experience with death yet but I know, and that is what the Officers warn us of during our lectures, that we could all be faced with it in the coming months ahead.

If I'm honest, I'll say I fall asleep sometimes when there is a lecture. Although we seem to get them often now so I have to pinch myself to keep from dozing off.

To change the subject, I am beginning to get quite used to my rifle which is great. I'm thinking that I am becoming a bit of a crack-shot at it.

I go to tell A.J., but I'm not allowed in the sick bay now, so I ask the doctor to tell A.J. that I am getting better at rifle practice and to tell him to hurry up and get strong again because I am way better than him now. He's really got some catching up to do.

The doctor looks at me with a fatherly expression on his face and closes the door behind him and puts his arm around my shoulder. We walk a little way away from the sick bay and he tells me that A.J. had a bad night and during the early hours of this morning had passed away quietly.

I was in a state of numbness. I just couldn't believe that he would die from this fever. Shocked is what I was. I found a corner to sit in, found some shade, and tried to take it in.

A.J. had been a good friend right from the very beginning when we had first met at Headquarters. We had started out on the same day and had stuck together ever since. I have other friends around me, but not like him. We were real mates together.

A thought suddenly popped into my mind, strangely, about the bloke in the train back in England. The train that started all this and took me from Evercreech to Bath. The man had said that it was alright to cry and let your feelings out.

So it just happened. Tears streamed along my face and no matter how I tried I couldn't hold them back. I couldn't catch my breath. I can't breathe. He was gone. A.J. was gone. Not from fighting a single fight either, but from some stupid infested mosquitoes. Damn it all; bloody hell. How can a person die from this, this malaria fever? I just couldn't get my head around it. So much for his inoculations I thought. What good did it do for him? Not one inoculation either. No, like me, A.J had several of them. This malaria fever has become our enemy too. The natives must be immune to it. I felt cold and shivers shoot through my whole body.

Later when I recovered a little from my grief, I was told that I could go see someone and talk about it if I felt the need. But I didn't. What could someone else do to help? A.J. was gone and I just had to face the fact and try and remember him like he would have wanted me to. It wasn't easy though, I can tell you.

I am not the only chap to go through this pain either. There are plenty others who see their friends go off to this other place, or have died.

I try to collect my thoughts and suddenly feel the urge to write a letter to my brother Tom.

I begin at first by letting him know how I am and what I've been getting up to and finally I decide to tell him of losing my friend A.J. and how he had died. I just felt like I needed to confide with someone and I knew he would read this and understand how I felt. I look up his address in a letter that Mum had sent to me. I start reading the part of Mum's letter again where she explains all about Tom. In June last year he had done all that was required of him and hadn't missed a single hit in his shooting trials. He had

Bill later received this photograph of the grave of A.J.
From the Regiment.

been called up on the 5th August and had gone straight to Winchester. He'd then had to go to Colchester and was then sent to the front, France.

I do have concerns for Tom and hope and pray that he will be alright.

I write out what I can of the address and hope it will find its way to him:

Private Tom Edwin Upshall
No.7290
1st Royal Hampshire Regiment
France

I take it straight over to the Post Room feeling good about writing to Tom and relieving some of the weight on my shoulders too. You see, I thought to myself, I need not talk to anyone here, I can write my thoughts down and share them with my own 'flesh and blood'.

I find myself taking extra care, from now on, to take more notice of our sanitary lectures and try to remember to keep myself covered. This is really hard though when the daily temperature is boiling hot and you start to sweat; you can't help but roll up your shirt sleeves or even take the shirt off completely.

On 2nd January Süleyman Askerî Bey assumed Mesopotamia Area Command. The Ottoman Army had no other resources during this time to move to this region, as other areas such as Gallipoli, the Caucasus and Palestine were of higher priority. Süleyman Askerî Bey wrote letters to Arab Sheiks asking them to fight against the British Army as he wanted to retake the Shatt-al-Arab region whatever the cost.

On 12th April Süleyman Askerî attacked the British camp at Shaiba. This was later known as the battle of Shaiba. He had around 4,000 regular troops and approximately 14,000 Arab irregulars. They attacked in the early hours of the morning. This proved to no avail. The Ottoman Infantry launched several attacks on the fortified British camp and later attempted another attack by bypassing it. When the British forced a counter attack, Süleyman Askerî retreated. The following day the British attacked his defensive positions. There were around 2,400 Ottoman men killed, wounded or taken prisoner. Süleyman Askerî was himself wounded at Shaiba. He later went on to shoot himself in the Baghdad hospital. Nureddin took over his command.

General Sir John Nixon was sent to command the British after their success and he ordered Charles V.F. Townsend to advance to Kut and if possible on to Baghdad. He successfully sustained attempts from the Ottoman Forces to halt his advances up the Tigris River.

By train to Madras and aboard S.S. Arankola to Andaman Islands

IT'S ***19TH JULY*** AND I have to leave Calicut. We are all going back to Bangalore but the Battalion has been put on a war footing. Oh I *am ready, we <u>all</u> are ready*. Come on and give us some action. The affects of the fever has put us in a different mood. I can't explain it exactly. I mean, it is not that we haven't been in a right frame of mind for war; it is just all the drilling, the training and the fact that for the last few months our first enemy has been a winged one that we cannot see until it's too late and nor can we fight it, we need to fight properly.

After spending around seven months in one place and for the most part being able to write and say '*I am having a fine time here*' is just not good enough, is it. I wanted more.

After the uncertainty of knowing our next destination, we are finally told that an enemy raid is expected on a group of Islands called the Andaman Islands and that we are to be sent there.

On ***22nd August*** we leave Bangalore headed towards *Madras*. Madras was on the eastern side of India. We were going to have to cross the country.

We were experiencing some really terrible thunderstorms. It seems that the locals are used to them here as it comes as part of the package, so to speak. Well that's what I heard anyhow. Honestly though, I have never heard such loud thunder as I've heard here the last weeks or so. It's quite frightening really; and I always thought it was bad enough back home.

At home when I was younger I used to want to hide under the stairs, but here, well, I probably would want to hide under a big forest leaf if I had half a chance. And when the rains stop, everywhere is practically flooding, so much falls in a matter of minutes!

Unfortunately for us we have to set out in a heavy rainfall, which we all reckon is going to last the whole day. As the temperature is well into the 80 degrees by now it's getting very humid. Steamy is a word I think of mostly. The soldiers in front of me look *steamy*!

It's pretty rough for all of us. The journey is tough and some of us are coming down with the shivers. I don't feel too bad myself yet but I could tell some chaps were having a bad time of it. We soon feel cold most of the time and our uniforms aren't drying on our bodies but instead they stick to you. At one stage I even put my coat on.

Luckily it isn't for long and we are glad to be on a train and taking in our surroundings. We are making our way through tropical rain forests with all manner of trees and plants. A lot I've never set eyes on before.

We also were seeing a lot more flat paddy fields on this side of India. But the main thing was the temperature. *Hot, very hot*. Sticky hot more like! It just made you feel darn sticky in all sorts of places!

A lot of chaps seem to have wounds that don't heal too, from scratching themselves too hard. I have a few wounds myself. It makes me think of Mum, not the wounds but the scratching. If she caught me scratching a bite on my arm or scratching my legs after walking into stinging nettles, she would shout so hard at me it would make me jump. "Bill", she'd shout, "you better stop that right now, or I'll give you something to scratch about meself, you hear me Bill?" "People will be a thinking you got fleas or the likes." The thought makes me smile. It's nice to suddenly have these things to think about. Funny how they can pop into your head, isn't it?

Talking of steam, as I was just a minute ago, we are permitted to let off some of our own for a while.

It takes us a whole day before we arrive in Madras. I must just say that the railway station here looks just like a palace. It has domes and lots of arches. But there is no time to get my camera out to capture this sight.

We leave Madras straight away and embark on the ***S.S. Arankola*** headed towards the *Andaman Islands*. Rumours have it that an enemy raid could be expected at any time. They are going to split us into two groups. One group will be stationed on Ross Island and the other on Aberdeen Island.

These groups would consist of two Battalions each; I was in the Battalion to go to *Port Blair* which was on Ross Island or so I believe as I find it very confusing when we are divided up and now I have forgotten which Island Port Blair is actually on! Anyway don't worry at least I know the place.

The boat journey to Port Blair is a welcome change to us all anyway. The *Arankola* is another great ship too. With two large funnels in its middle it steams away to take us on our next destination. We are on the Bay of Bengal (I asked a sergeant). Yes, I am beginning to find my confidence. After losing A.J, I have had to speak up for myself more. I still am trying to get used to it though, but I will.

It's nice to have a bit of sea air during the day too, as this heat can be too much at times. It is quite a journey to these Islands. It's been two days and we still haven't got there yet. Half the time I don't seem to be able to focus on the day or I forget which day it is, until someone reminds me of it.

The going was rough too. Who would have thought it? It gets rough on the water though when the rains come and we all got sea-sick again, mores' the pity.

As we get nearer to the Andaman Islands I notice that there are more than two islands but many of them.

On approaching Port Blair I look up and could see our Barracks as they were right on a small hill, and I thought at first that they were somebody's grand home, as it didn't really look like a Barracks, much too grand I thought. But as it turned out, this was to be our new Barracks.

I'm not sure what the trouble is and neither does anyone else, but we have to sleep another night on board, even though we've reached Port Blair.

A Private comes around handing out our mail. This was a pleasant surprise. It must have been put on the ship at Madras I suppose.

I am very pleased to hear my name called out and can't wait to read it and to catch up with everything going on in Evercreech. It does us all so good to be able to keep in touch with our families. We are all of us so happy and grateful when our names get called and an envelope or card gets thrown in our direction. Not all of us are lucky enough to have mail though. It differs. I sometimes don't have anything to read while maybe others do. You never know when you will get lucky. It's really quite exciting when I think about it. It's a bit like having Christmas over and over again.

I GET A LETTER: MY BROTHER TOM HAS BEEN KILLED

I CATCH MY LETTER and move to one side and find a little corner to crouch into. I've only got the one letter from home but it does contain a card as well. It was to wish me another happy birthday. Quite frankly I hadn't given it a second thought, but now I was 18 years old! I shrugged it off and start to read what Mum has written, getting interrupted by my neighbour as he starts laughing out loud about something that's tickled him. I shift a bit and read again, taking all the news and gossip in. Then I turn to the next page.

Mum says on the first page, "Bill I gotta tell ye somethin..."

But when I turn the page and start to read on I start to shake. "Hey, you alright there buddy?" asks my neighbouring soldier, I can't remember his name. I look him in the eyes and mine go all blurry, "my brother Tom has been killed," I just about manage to say. He lays his hand on my shoulder and squeezes just a little. Then he stands up and crouches in front of me, grabs my coat that I had taken off earlier on, and drapes it around me, pulling it tight at the front and buttoning it up under my chin. "There you go lad, that'll help the shivering." He leaves me alone.

Tom only got to be 29 years old. Oh god, I just can't believe I'm hearing this. I feel sick. He has two children for pity's sake and now they have lost their dad. And Ada, his wife, what must she be going through right now? Mum writes:

> *"That lovely wife of his is beside 'erself wi grief en I hopes to God she don't goin make erself ill, what wi copin wi the two little uns an all. The poor lasses won't ave a father to bring em up now."*

Why hadn't he come over to India? But then I reckon he wouldn't have had much of a choice when he had recruited as to which place or country to go to, would he? He was in the Hampshire Regiment and was called up after I came here, I remember.

Mum goes on to explain how he had landed up being sent over to Belgium. I looked away from the letter thinking and worrying if he'd ever gotten my letter as I'd put France on it. Silly to think of a thing like that as it doesn't really make any difference now does it. But then I again if he had gotten it, he would at least have known that I was thinking of him.

He was killed at the battle at Ypres. That is where he had lost his life for England. Ypres, Belgium. Then I look at the date Mum has written: 13th May 1915. That's three months ago now.

Not long after A.J. had died. Mum had put a newspaper cutting in with her letter and this is what it said:

> DISTINCTION FOR AN EVERCREECH MAN AT THE FRONT
>
> Private Upshall, of the 1st Hants Regiment writes to his wife at Evercreech as follows:-
>
> "We had beer and plenty of good things at Christmas, and are having a rest now. We had a truce with the Germans in front of us for Christmas. I gave one The News of the World newspaper. He could speak English. It seemed funny for us and the Germans out shaking hands with one another, now trying to shoot one another again. I have been mentioned in Dispatches for bravery, and I have had this card (enclosed) from the General."
>
> The card is worded as follows:- "Fourth Division, British Expeditionary Force. No.7290 Pte. T. Upshall, 1st Hants Regt. Your Commanding Officer and Brigade Commander have informed me that you have distinguished yourself by conspicuous bravery in the field. I have read their report with much pleasure. – H.F.M. WILSON, Major-General, Commanding 4th Division."

Mum continues to write that both she and Dad are in a terrible state and are just beyond themselves worrying about me. In fact Mum says, "Bill I am a wishing yer could be a comin home to me son."

My eyes well up and I feel a tear run down my cheek. Followed by more tears, I am just so overwhelmed by it all. I wipe them away as quick as I can but more come in their place. I need some air and then realise I am sat on the deck of a ship, in the air.

I shall have to write and tell Mum that I am safe where I am at the moment and to "please don't worry too much". I feel so scared right now and that big old knot has returned in the pit of my stomach.

Tom Edwin Upshall, 1st Hants Regiment.

Now I just hope that Mum and Dad take care not to worry about me and to look after themselves. I'll ask them to do this when I write soon, not that they'll take a blind bit of notice.

After the Tattoo and Guard mounting is over I stay on the bow of the ship looking out across the water.

One thing I've noticed about myself since being so far away from home is that I seem to *act different*. I don't know whether it's my imagination or not, but I feel different. We all feel different. Other chaps have mentioned it too.

Hmm, I smile to myself for this, but I've just had a thought: *we are different – we've got darker skin from the sun!* One Sergeant said to me, joking of course; "my boy, you're almost a white native now, you know!"

The Last Post suddenly starts playing. Christ didn't that make me jump out my skin. I stand and listen to it. I listen like I hear it for the first time. The bugle's notes penetrate deep into my skin. It feels consoling. I think of Tom and his death as I hang on to every single one of those notes. I am standing to attention and I pray that he has not suffered and has now found a resting place. Oh my God the bugle sounds so beautiful and yet so sad.

I don't sleep very well that night. In fact, at one stage I wake up in a sweat. Did Tom ever receive my letter that I had sent to him? Would he have read it? Did it get to him before he...?

I got myself in a real old 'pickle'. When I finally got back to sleep, it was almost time to get up. I'd been dreaming all sorts of horrible scenes of Germans laughing at me, reading a newspaper. Of Tom getting killed and calling me and I was running somewhere soaking wet... My head was aching and I felt quite sick.

Our new Barracks at Port Blair

AT 9 AM ON ***27th August*** we step foot on the Andaman Islands, *Port Blair*. The Battalion stands ready for inspection.

We have already been informed that we are put in a state of defence. The possibility of an enemy raid is one reason, which we've already been told about; but when we hear that on this island there are about 10,000 convicts, it makes us all feel a little nervy to say the least. To hear, as well, that the convicts were virtually free to walk the islands whenever they wanted, well that was like rubbing salt in your wound, which is what that was.

Some convicts were allotted later as servants to the Officers. *Blimey*. I bet they were pleased to hear that! Good luck with that one chaps. I don't think I'd like one buzzing around me, even if he was my servant. Oh, the Officers explained to us how it would be a *unique* experience for us all. Unique my aunt fanny! It sounds ridiculous to me. I tell you what though, I shall be avoiding any eye contact with any of them, you bet, even if they do appear friendly.

My Dad's words popped right into my head: 'never trust a bad'un', that's what he'd say. (Not to trust a bad one, he meant).

"A Unique experience"? What the bloody hell is he thinking about giving us a chance to see murderers roaming the islands free? What the hell is going on here?" one chap starts to mumble and moan and groan. I thought, shall I let him know that I was just thinking the very same thoughts. But that's the trouble with me and always has been, I only *think* these thoughts and someone else comes out and says them!

We spend the next couple of days trying to settle in and put our minds at ease.

Parades are at 6.30 a.m. as usual. We are permitted to parade in our shirtsleeves and rifles.

We are disciplined about bathing. You can hardly blame us for wanting to, being on an island. A tropical island no less and looking at water that is just so tempting when the heat has just been turned up a notch higher! We are, however, not permitted to bathe before 5 p.m. Also we *have* to wear bathing drawers.

Some days it is just so hot that by midday even the officers just tell us to rest. We do our drilling and marching as early as possible and then it's too hot to move.

This is when boredom can be a bit of a pain. Don't get me wrong when I say we are glad not to march or have to do any chores, but after so many days it gets boring. The day drags on. I would rather be doing things. When I'm not doing anything my mind starts to wander and I get to thinking about all sorts. I think of Tom and I think of Mum and Dad and I think of my friends. I don´t much like it at all.

And where is this enemy that's supposed to attack?

When we'd arrived at the camp we knew that this was an island that the English army were occupying, because of other battalions that we could see there.

The doctor in charge here is concerned about the wounds on us. They're not getting better. A scratch seems to turn nasty. He's afraid of some of us getting blood poisoning, he says.

We all get a lecture on hygiene. And we are told time and time again that we mustn't scratch with dirty hands. In fact, we get inspections now to check if we keep clean!

We're drilled hard even though we're all on an island. But I suppose we do have to all keep ourselves fit. The doctor tells us that it is to our "best advantage" that we try and all take part in our drilling because that way we will stay strong and not get weak. It seems though that each week the number of chaps getting fever is creeping up. To tell you the truth I am worried I might get it too.

After breakfast, by which time we are starving, a small group of us decide to go for a walk and look around. The water is lovely by the shore. It is so blue, (it sometimes looks green) and so clear you can see the bottom. One chap starts undressing, then another joins in and before you know it we are all undressed and in the water. Dare I say it but we do go in stark naked. It's such a relief to feel warm water over your body, especially if some of us still have some bad scratches. We have to be careful not to stay in too long though, which is so easy to do being as it's so warm.

I know what you're all thinking... we weren't supposed to bathe until 5p.m. Well, that's the beauty of some parts of the island. When there is just nobody else about, we just can't help ourselves. We are quick too. Blimey I've never undressed so quick in all my life. There is the element of excitement too. Knowing darn well that it's not allowed this time of the day (not sure why) and doing it anyway. We are in the water, a quick swim and we're out again, before you can say 'Jack Robinson'. I am sure, though, if we got caught we'd get a damn good telling-off.

If the rains are coming though, we soon leave shore! And be quick to get all our clothes on, as when it comes, the rain is like a heavy sheet falling. It soon cools down as well after the rain. When we've got inside our barracks and it starts to rain, it's like a load of soldiers marching like the clappers on top of the roof, it's so loud.

Some days of the week we have to leave the island by a small rowing boat and head off to Aberdeen Island with A Company and we practice entrenching, also tent pitching. I reckon by the time we've had all this practice and we get sent to fight the enemy we shall all be as prepared as we can be.

Thursday we get a day off and some of us decide to go off and explore.

I get as close as I can to some elephants that we see roaming the forest not far from our barracks. They are really enormous animals and very strong. But when they eat using their long trunks they seem to do it carefully and it's to me quite a mind boggling experience.

Shall I also mention that we were told to keep our wits about us when advancing around the island and also to always travel in groups? Why? Well, only because we might suddenly come across a murderer or some other dangerous criminal. You see if you remember I mentioned the convicts that are settled here and that they were somehow allowed to walk about, well, virtually free so to speak. Thanks for the warning chaps!

We come across some natives carrying baskets and go over to them to see what they have inside the baskets. We're curious like that! Well, I'm glad we did get to look, as they had some shells amongst other things.

The shells were really big. In fact I have never seen such shells as these before. They were all shiny too. I made a gesture that I wanted to have a better look at one and maybe, well, can I touch it and pick it up? I asked one of the natives. He smiled at me, mumbled something to another, had a bit of a laugh and he put down his basket and picked one of the shells up and handed it to me. He made a gesture that I should hold it up to the light, which I did. On the shiny part, if I held it and moved it back and forth I could see all different colours coming through. This is great, I thought. I wanted one of these. It didn't even dawn on me that these natives could have been convicts, but as it turns out, they weren't. I still couldn't get my head around the fact that they all roamed the Islands.

Some parts of the islands looked real creepy to me too. There were strange trees where the roots showed above the ground. Some would even been wrapped around a stone or an abandoned ruin. No, I kept pretty much near familiar parts myself.

The strange trees had so an impression on my mind that later on when I was back in our barracks, I just had to find out more about them. Apparently these unusual trees are called Banyan Trees and the roots were quite normal for this particular tree and when the roots eventually reach the ground they turn into trees themselves. How strange is that? Blimey no wonder they could take over whole patches of ground.

If you are wondering about my camera as well, then don't worry I did still have it safely tucked away. I just didn't fancy bringing it out in the open around here.

There were guards all around though, don't get me wrong.

Assignments were regularly given to us for both the Ross Island and the Aberdeen Island. We had boats to travel to and from the Islands.

Guess what? That afternoon when we finally walked back to our barracks I had in my rucksack two lovely big shells! They turned out to be Mother of Pearl too, which I hadn't realised until this was pointed out to me. I just bought them because they looked really nice.

I manage to have the shells packed up and sent back to England to my mum, as one of the Officers happens to have a crate ready to send to his parents in nearby Castle Cary. How about that. What a coincidence. I feel really very lucky. It will be a nice gesture to cheer up Mum too I think.

Although being amongst convicts on a tropical island, we were soldiers and were here to stay as such, and this was not to be thought of in any other way. Our typical weeks programme was strict as it had always been.

I have Malaria Fever and leave the Islands

The heavy rains and getting wet and the drastic changes in temperature have got the better of me I reckon. The last few months have been tough and around 60 inches of rain has fallen. The Islands seem suddenly not such a nice place to be. It's not healthy anymore. Many chaps have fallen ill with malaria fever.

You know the saying 'dropping like flies', well that's suddenly what seemed to occur on the island. I am unfortunate enough to be among the men dropping. On ***16th October*** I get admitted to Port Blair hospital with suspected malaria fever. The Doctor had been giving us all doses of quinine against the fever every so often, but despite this I think I've caught it. I am not sure if it's the quinine or the fever, but my eyes have gone blurry and I feel as though I'm all over the place. I can't stand up for too long without wobbling. Blimey, now what will happen to me?

After staying in the sick bay for what seemed like a few days, the Doctor came over to me. Oh, I think to myself, is he bearing good or bad news? Am I going to die just like A.J.? He says, "Bill, I am discharging you." Whew, that was close. "You are not out of the woods yet though Bill, hang on a minute and listen carefully." He went on to explain that he is going to send me to a place called Wellington, along with a group of other chaps that were able to make the journey, and that we would be allowed to stay there to recuperate and get fit again. He asks me how I'd feel about that idea. I just nod my head in agreement.

Blimey what a relief that was to me I can say, I feel as though I would agree to almost any suggestion right now as I am not in a good place, mind or body wise. God bless you A.J. but I am not ready to come and join you just yet, if it's all the same to you, thank you very much.

The enemy raid that was expected never came to anything either. You could hear the sound of guns away in the distance across the sea, but that was about it. I wasn't about to miss out on any immediate action, and the thought of leaving here to recuperate felt as a bit of a relief as you might agree.

Colonel Clutterbuck has also been taken sick and there are rumours that he might be joining us.

On ***6th November,*** I am among a group of many men, including an Officer who has to depart the Andaman Islands and cross back to Madras on the S.S. "Maharaja" (another fine ship, I might add although I wasn't quite up to enjoying the journey.)

We were all heading to *Wellington*. It is a place up in the hills where detachments of convalescents and young soldiers are sent. It has a much better climate too, apparently. Or so we are led to believe. From Madras we set out by rail.

Colonel Clutterbuck wasn't among us but had been sent back home on leave.

I can't recall much of the first part of our train journey as I dosed in and out of sleep for most of it. The last part, however, I did take a bit more notice of. Partly due to the way the train was rattling and puffing as it weaved its way through hilltops and cliffs. Some of the cliff drops were a bit distressing to say the least. But the views, when I caught glimpses between patches of mist, were quite amazing. The air seemed to feel different as well. I had a good feeling about this place.

The 'hospital' was very impressive. The buildings consisted of endless arches below and long balconies with pillars above. It looked more like a grand hotel than a hospital.

My recovery at Wellington

THE FOLLOWING WEEKS SEEMED to pass and they turned into months. I was apparently pretty rough at one stage. There is hardly anything of it that I can remember. I recall shivering a lot and sweating. Sometimes I would wake up and feel like I was led in water, I would sweat so badly.

When I feel up to it I start to open some mail that has been left for me. I had a Christmas card from the family back in Evercreech and a letter from Mum.

She writes that Jesse has 'tied the knot' (which brings a smile to my cheeks) and gotten married to his sweetheart Emma Hiscox. They married in a place called Pilton in Somerset, which is a village very close to Evercreech, on 17th November 1915.

It's a shame I couldn't have been there to see the wedding but never mind, I hope they will be very happy. I am pleased for him.

She goes on to write that he wanted to marry before having to go into the army, which has been inevitable and he has, unfortunately, had to sign up.

On ***22nd November*** Townsend and Nureddin fought at the battle of Ctesiphon, which was 25miles south of Baghdad. A Battle which lasted 5 long days and became a stalemate as it resulted in

both parties having to retreat. Townsend ordered his troops back to Kut-al-Amara. Nureddin encircled the British troops and ordered more troops to march down the river.
Thus on 7th December the siege of Kut began. The British defended Kut but were cut off from further supplies. Attempts to send through relief forces failed and the British forces received only small quantities of supplies by air. Nureddin was replaced by a German General Halil Kut. He forced the British to choose between starving or surrendering.

❖ ❖ ❖

1916

Eventually we all seem to be getting back our health and feeling much brighter. What a relief. A new year has begun and we are catching up on some rifle practice and parading again. Basically we are all very much on our way to a recovery; many of us, me included, are wondering when we will be reunited with our battalions again.

But until that time comes I am making the most of my stay here and I am very thankful that I have been well enough to travel to this hospital. Now I have had the chance to get a good look at the place and its surroundings, it most probably was a Hotel once, before the British took over it.

The clearer air has done us all the world of good.

Dr. Bishop, whom we had to look after us all, was a very good, kind and considerate Doctor. He looked after us well and it was probably due to his care and attention that we all recovered from this disease so quickly and were ready for action once more.

I thought, at the time, what a good surname to have when your main job is to take care of soldiers who are going to war! You get what I mean by that don't you? 'Bishop', healing us back to health! He lived up to his surname.

My new Barracks at Dinapore

On ***4th February*** the fit and eager soldiers amongst us are ready to leave Wellington and we now find ourselves heading to *Dinapore,* to be reunited with our Battalions there. They have already left the Andaman Islands and had sailed to *Calcutta* in January and from there on to Dinapore.

It gets very cold here in Dinapore at night and also in the mornings but we are told that we will have to get used to the temperature becoming even hotter during daytime than we've probably been used to. In fact, the nights are so darn cold here that we all need extra thick blankets to sleep under and in the mornings it's so cold that we've all found it best if we just put on as many layers of clothing as we possibly have amongst our kit, or we'll just damn shiver our way to inspection! This is, of course, a blessed nuisance because as the day progresses we then find we have to shed a layer or two, time permitting, or stick and sweat the rest of the day! Blimey talk about extremes.

Another thing about Dinapore is the dust. We have all experienced it. For example, if whilst we're drilling along the road and some form of transport were to pass us by, it leaves a form of floating dust in the air for what seems like ages; like a very low cloud hanging over it. You can hardly see in front of you and not only that but it makes my throat feel very dry and it settles on our clothes. And it's only February!

Did I say about it being flat? Well, it is. After being up in the hills and then coming to here where it's just the opposite, I had to ask if we had gone over into another country! It's like you can see for miles. I'm glad there are lots of trees though, because that makes it feel a bit safer.

The barracks are very close to a river; built along a river is really a better description. And further along, the river joins the biggest river I have ever seen in my life and the biggest, I think, anyone else has ever seen. It's called The Ganges.

You could fit the whole of Evercreech across this river and still have room to spare! It's vast!

Have I mentioned the pith helmets? Well, now I am pleased to have one and realise there full function. After having malaria fever I have felt a bit vulnerable towards the heat, and the helmet shades the sun very well. It's handy if it rains too, as the brim of the helmet holds back the rain. A handy tip, which I was shown, was to dunk the helmet in water, drain it off and put it on your head. It will keep you cool for a while. A puggaree goes around the helmet and this is like a linen cloth really which is very handy against any of those nasty mosquitoes. Don't ask me why it's called a puggaree because I can't tell you that.

Despite it being very dusty, the good things about Dinapore are the vegetables. They seem to grow lots of vegetables here. This has the advantage of making the place feel a lot more homely. It reminds me of my father's vegetable patches at home. My dad likes his vegetables. I like *his* vegetables. I like these vegetables too. Although having said that I have heard that now the hotter weather is approaching these vegetables will get scarce. In fact we are rationed to 14 ounces of vegetables per man. They don't have potatoes though. But they grow rice here instead. Rice is what the people here are used to growing. There are lots of people living here too in this part.

The Barracks here seem to be like a permanent Department for the Military. We have been building up these last few weeks for some kind of special training too. A lot of marching is what we've been doing. Also we have to get up at the crack of dawn, in the freezing cold weather, and then parading. We do lots of Drilling. The Officers are making fitter soldiers of us I reckon.

We learn new tactics. The training seems to be for all sorts of possible attacks and manoeuvres. We all return to our Barracks completely exhausted by the afternoon and have to sleep it off!

I do my best to maintain my webbing equipment. Not that I have a lot of choice. We are all expected to keep even the buckles polished and looking tip top. At least whilst we are back in the Barracks anyhow. It makes sense though, to take care of the equipment, otherwise I will have nowhere to keep all my kit, especially my water bottle. We do have the Tailors if any part needs repairing though.

I can't help but think it will soon be our time to relieve a fighting Battalion somewhere or another. Just the way our training has been stepped up a notch and the fact that some of us are being taught how to cook dinners in kettles. I say this because on Fridays now when we are still out in the trenches this is what happens. We get our meals in the trenches which I guess would have been the situation where Tom had been, but for us this is new.

On Thursday ***10th February*** at 6.30a.m we report for parade as usual, except that we have to carry our greatcoats with us!

Later that morning we all have to parade outside the Orderly Room and have been given dummy cartridges as we are to be tested in rapid loading techniques. Our pouches are also examined, just in case anybody has had other ideas and might have ball ammunition with them! I'm guessing, of course.

We are to attend a Course of Musketry at Rawalpindi and are told that we will leave on the 13th at 10.11a.m.

On the morning of the ***12th*** I and a couple of friends catch sight of a Notice which has been put up that mentions a performance which will be given by the "George" Bioscope Company in the Theatre for all soldiers wishing to attend.

Now I'll let you in to a little secret; I have always been a bit of a quiet one but on certain occasions do enjoy dressing up with fellow colleagues and having a downright good old laugh.

I can't explain why we looked at each other that day like we did but we were going to have a laugh. I'd gotten through a rough time lately and so had the other chaps and we just felt an urge coming on to do something a bit out of the ordinary.

My performance in "The Early Birds"

There were six of us in all and we confronted one of the Theatre Company of our little surprise and he thought it would be a great idea.

He showed us into a nearby tent and we started working out a routine and searching for some comical clothing to wear. I was trying to turn a sheet into a skirt, when a member of the Theatre

Company came in to see how we were getting on. He showed us some outfits they had with them which might be of use to us and left.

Henry, who was one of our team, asked if he could use the sheet as he'd give me the honour of dressing as a woman. Well that was decided then but I didn't mind one bit. He pulled and tugged at that sheet until he had a long shirt and then he wrote 'I am Henry VIII' on it!

Samuel had found a pointed hat like jesters wore and had written 'sawdust' across a bit of sheet and stuck it on the front of the hat.

By the time we had all completely finished with our costumes, we had also been going over a routine and a little sing song act.

Walter started us off as we walked right back into the barracks where all the chaps were still sitting about and chatting away. He started with, what I thought later to be rather suitable because of the noise at the time, the 'early birds' song. I didn't actually know the words to it, so I pranced about to his words. Thankfully he only did two verses of that song and we were off on the next one...' It's a long way to Tipperary', which everybody joined in with. Then Arthur and I, who were also dressed similar, started singing 'Hold your hand out naughty boy'.

We finished our routine with 'Pack up your troubles in your old kit bag' and our ultimate song was 'We'll never let the old flag fall', which brought everyone into motion stamping their feet at the appropriate chorus and drumming away on just about anything, with just about anything. All in all it was just a bit of a laugh to finish a really good day and I reckon we were a hit!

The whole act didn't last all that long really and afterwards we all enjoyed the Bioscope performance. It was a good night and I slept the best ever.

We even had our photographs taken by the Company before we discarded our costumes. So our little act has been captured and I can treasure the moment of madness in years to come! Each of us got given a copy for a keepsake.

On ***29th February*** the Battalion undergoes the 'Kitchener's Test'. This was more like an endurance test I reckon and it meant that for four days and nights we find ourselves marching up and down and across land amounting to about 120 miles in distance and camping out in trenches. Oh, now I realise what that was all about earlier on in the month; it was probably preparing us for this.

Talk about getting sore feet. Boy did I ever have sore feet. Not to mention getting drenched at night. Anyhow, we were well rewarded, as we all passed the test. Not bad going Bill, I thought, considering I was so sick not all too long ago. We were all given a great deal of credit for our efforts.

It's the end of February and we all get Christmas Presents! Apparently the mail boat was late.

We had all come back from Sunday Church Parade and were all gathered around for the handing out of belated Christmas gifts.

The gifts turned out to be from Princess Mary. Well, I personally felt quite honoured myself for this unexpected gesture.

What we all had given us was a little brass tin. Well, I say little, but it would only just fit in my breast pocket.

Inside is a small Christmas card from the Princess Mary, which says the following:

With best wishes
for a
victorious
New Year

From
the Princess Mary
and friends at
home.

1916 "The Early Birds" I am sat on the left in the front row!

And do you know what else was in that box? There were two packets: one packet of tobacco and another packet of cigarettes.

This had also been very carefully thought out, because those amongst us who didn't smoke received chocolate.

There was also a *Silver Bullet*! I am not kidding there is actually a Silver Bullet. Not just any old bullet either. It's a bullet that has been cleverly made into a pencil holder! I must have said the word bullet out loud because then some clever chap says it's not a real bullet. Well of course it isn't, actually it is the cartridge case of a bullet, but to me it looks like a bullet.

I shall treasure this gift forever and make real sure that I look after this until I am old and grey and can pass it on to my own son when the time comes. Blimey. This is just great. No, I mean it; seriously, this is a real nice gift to have. I love it. We *all love it.*

Did I ever mention my pencil? I don't think I did. Pencil? You probably are asking yourself. Why should he mention such a minute detail? Well, actually, it is of some importance. The pencil is not just an ordinary pencil. It writes in purple! Yes you heard, *purple*. Why this colour I suppose you're asking yourself next? Well, it is said that this colour will not fade like a normal pencil colour.

Of course my bullet had real purpose now. I pushed my purple pencil into it, as far up as I could push it and it fitted nicely. It felt better in my hand to write with this now as the pencil was only a very small one.

What an idea this was. Thank you to whoever was responsible for this great idea.

I think that last gruelling exercise has done me no good, as I am admitted into the camps Hospital on ***27th February.***

Luckily for me though, I only needed a bit of tender loving care!

After just under a week, I am discharged again. ***(6th March)***

I was not the only one either, there were many more chaps who probably hadn't fully recovered from the first time. As quick as the hospital was getting us fitter ones discharged; new casualties were being admitted.

A CHOLERA OUTBREAK: I GET SENT TO DARJEELING

AS WE GO INTO April it gets even hotter, with temperatures reaching over 100 degrees towards midday!

But dust storms; well, I had never seen anything like it in my life. We couldn't train or do much of anything when one came. Instead we would be making a mad dash for the barracks and the ones closest to the windows would shut them tight as quickly as they could. It was not only against the dust but because of the wind. Not forgetting it kept the heat outside instead of inside the barracks too.

Those times were a blessed nuisance, as one Officer kept mentioning. Why? Because from 9a.m until 4p.m. all of us men had to stay indoors!

Oh, you might think to yourself, well that can't be too bad. No training or exercising or drilling to do. And you'd be right in thinking this, as did we in the beginning. But you see, after so many days, this just quite frankly becomes monotonous to say the least, and that's putting it politely too!

Oh, we didn't complain though. We didn't grumble at all. There was, with a bit of thought, enough you could find to do during this time. Some would play cards; others would re-read previous letters or writing new letters to friends and relatives back home.

I write to my sister Laura, who is in service in Exeter and will be 22 in September. I know I am jumping the gun a bit, but considering how long it took our Christmas Gifts to reach us, I figure best be sooner rather than later. Who knows what or where I might be a few months on down the line?

Cleaning our gear was, of course, a *must do job*.

I get a letter from my brother Frederick and he has 'tied the knot' he says which has pleased Mum and Dad. He has married his Elizabeth, he says and they were married in March of this year in West Ham, London. What is it with my brothers lately all getting married? He goes on to say that he will most likely be going to France soon.

I decided to volunteer for a Gymnasium Class when the opportunity arose, which also kept me busy for three days in the week. The idea being, that while keeping fit I could get myself into a bit of shape. Also now I'd read about Fred possibly going over to France, well, quite frankly I was angry for some reason. All I could think of was that if he did go to France, would he come out of it alright?

With July now here, we have the monsoon to cope with. This was to our advantage however, as it stopped the dust; which was good. Well and truly dampened down was the dust. Also suddenly everything turned amazingly green!

Whilst we were marching through the Banikpur neighbourhood there was a lot of unrest there which felt very uneasy and we were relieved to get back to Dinapore.

Later though there was another shock for all of us troops, when we were to discover, would you believe it, the Battalion was affected with Cholera. I got so worked up about this bad news as I reckoned I could be a likely candidate to fall ill with it, seeing as I'd been in a bit of trouble before and didn't know whether I had enough strength to come through this if it spread amongst us.

Naturally when the Medical team had discovered the fever, everybody had a lecture on not drinking the local water, unless it had been boiled beforehand. And all foods had to be well cooked and utensils boiled before use. The Officers in charge had all done their best to make sure this happened and regularly inspected the cookhouses. Not forgetting the latrines, they were checked too and everyone had been lectured on washing hands as frequent as possible.

Any signs from us of bowel trouble or diarrhoea were to be reported to the medical team immediately.

On ***19th July*** the unfortunate groups of men from each Battalion who are showing signs of the disease are to be sent to a place called *Darjeeling*.

I happen to be one of those unfortunate men. Didn't I expect this? Well I did but I had secretly hoped I'd get lucky this time around, but it wasn't to be.

Just like at Wellington, there is also a large hospital here. We arrive by train, which was a magnificent journey by the way.

I do not feel happy about being sent away from my Battalion once more, however I make up my mind to take this opportunity that I am given by getting myself fit and well enough again. I can't help thinking maybe I would be sent home if I don't recover this time around and I wasn't planning on going home just yet.

The journey to Darjeeling was something else. At one stage we had to cross the Lower Ganges on a bridge called Sara. When I mentioned in the very beginning of my story the wonders of the viaducts in Somerset, I would never have dreamed I would right now be travelling on a steam train towards the Himalayans.

At one stage of the journey we had to change over to a smaller gauge railway.

Another difference in the trains, which I have forgotten to mention before, is the fact that the seats on the carriages face lengthways instead of facing towards the front. There are racks under the seats where we can put our rifles and racks overhead which we use for our kit bags.

As we travelled further up the steep mountains there were spirals and zigzags and if I looked out the window the end coach could actually see the front engine!

I am actually enjoying it up here in the hills. It's so much cooler here that we all seem to revive from it. The air seems fresher, even though back at Dinajpur, after a rainfall the air was fresh, up here it seems twice as fresh again. I suppose, naturally, we are a lot more shaded by the steep hills and all the trees which surround the hospital here.

In the early mornings the valley gets enshrouded in mist. I've never experienced anything like it before.

We are all recovering quite rapidly and this is pleasing the Officers in charge.

I have had a grand time up here in the hills and I was sorry to hear that we were all going to be leaving shortly.

On ***29th August*** we find ourselves travelling back down the hills towards *Dinajpur* again. But do you know what? I did feel well enough and quite frankly I was rather relieved to be heading back down to rejoin our Battalion, than being sent home without seeing even anything remotely resembling a battle.

The Monsoon was apparently quite bad here last month and, they tell us, that there had been so much rain here it had caused some very serious landslides. In fact, there had been one bad landslide that had completely blocked the railway going up to the hills, and had also delayed a group of men who were at the time, making their way back to Dinajpur!

We've heard from an Officer that the Ganges has broken its banks and caused the river to flow over.

I don't know; one minute we are trying to cope with so much dust you can hardly breathe, and the next there is just so much rain it's unbelievable and the place gets swamped. No wonder there are so many of us becoming ill! Who wouldn't in these sorts of conditions?

But then, I am quite ashamed to be grumbling when I hear of the horrors our fellow soldiers are having to cope with back in France and Belgium. It doesn't bear thinking about. I feel so sorry for them. But what can I do? I can't help it that I was sent over here to India. I still don't know what we are all to expect further on. I get so confused with all of this but I feel sure we're being kept in training for the purpose of relieving our fellow troops somewhere else.

The following week I find myself one of many men who are given good conduct badges! Now I know you are itching to know what for. This is the thing; I'm not exactly sure what I've earned it for. Probably the heavy training we had undergone the month earlier. I might have missed the explanation though when I got sent to Darjeeling. There are hundreds of us that are given this anyway and I feel proud to have it and that's that.

When I say 'badge', well, it is not exactly one as such, more a stripe with a point in the middle that we get to have sewn onto our jacket sleeve. Apparently you can earn more than one of these.

It seems a lot of men have been sent off to other places in India. Whether it's to do some sort of special training under certain weather conditions or whether it's to fight the Turks, I don't know. As troops leave here many new troops seem to take their place. It's a mass unit of activity is what it is.

Maybe something is in the planning. I say this because we have just of lately been doing some night operations, which we haven't done before.

After being in the hills it seems still very hot here.

As we go from September into October the temperature seems to drop at a dramatic pace. I say this because, before we all know what's hit us, we're turning all the fans out and putting on extra layers of clothing! At night I hardly know how to keep warm. Talk about a change.

However it does bring the best out in all of us, as our Officers begin to notice.

The coolness makes us feel a lot sharper and more alert, which is good. Also we all feel loads fitter. I mean to say we all feel a lot healthier and stronger. I must speak for myself, but notice it in the other lads too, that I have a bigger appetite. This has got to be a good sign.

I get another letter from Mum, so when I get the chance after eating, I find a quiet spot and start to read. It's your typical letter really and Mum's let me in on all the latest bits of family news that she writes to cheer me up, she says. Kate has had another baby girl and calls her Phyllis. Jesse and Emma have a little boy called Frederick and Mum goes on to explain about her cousin Christopher getting married to Lily in Bagber and what a lovely day that was in April. I stop reading to try and take it all in and can't quite remember which cousin she's talking about. Frankly with all my brothers and sisters to keep track of, anyone not directly involved just skips my memory.

On ***24th April*** attempts by the British to send reinforcements to Townsend in Kut by way of a paddle steamer down river also failed. Townsend attempted to break through the Ottoman attacks rather than await further supplies but on ***29th April*** he was forced to surrender. British soldiers, 13,164 in all, became captives of the Ottoman Army. All British commanders involved in rescuing Townsend were relieved of their duties and the British were humiliated by their failure. They had already been defeated at Gallipoli 4 months prior to this.

There was a major problem with all British ships entering Basra as there was no logical way to move supplies further inland. Ships had to wait sometimes for days on end to be unloaded. The supplies had to be then loaded onto a steamer to travel up river, or put into warehouses. These warehouses soon exhausted their space. The British had previously asked the Indian Government to build a railway but this had at first been rejected, but after the siege of Kut this plan was approved. The British improved the Port at Basra enabling ships to unload efficiently and good roads were built. Rest Camps and supply dumps were also created to receive materials for the troops. New Hospitals were also built to care for the wounded and the sick. This resulted in the British being able to bring more troops and equipment into the area and to the front lines.

ABOARD THE S.S. ELLENGA TO MESOPOTAMIA

WE'VE ALL BEEN ASKED to fall in at the main barrack for a lecture. But when we have settled down, the Colonel starts talking and asks for volunteers to go to Mesopotamia.

Fit men were wanted as reinforcements in Mesopotamia.

We would be an addition to the 3rd Indian Division based at Basra. Those going will be called the Mesopotamia Expeditionary Force.

Well I wanted a change of scenery, so now is my chance, I think to myself. Oh, I know what you're thinking now. Change of scenery Bill, it seems like that's about all you have been doing. But hang on a minute here; do you realise that Mesopotamia is another country altogether. That's what I'm talking about. I need out of this 'hot-one-minute, cold-the-next; monsoon- weather-country' we are in! We all think pretty much the same. So we all volunteer; men are chosen from each of the Companies. I can't explain how pleased I feel when I do get picked to go.

This will be another long journey ahead.

All in all 300 of us pack our gear and get ready to leave Dinajpur.

On ***21st October*** we embark and sail on the S.S. *Ellenga*. This ship looks a lot heavier than the previous ones and I can't wait to get on board. I feel the same sort of rush go through my body as when I left Southampton. Blimey, that seems ages ago now I think about it. Our kit bags are stowed away, except for our blankets, overcoats and rifles. We are allowed to access our bags twice a week though for a change of clothes.

We travel through the mouth of the Ganges and into the Bay of Bengal. Along the East Coast of India and pass the southern tip and travel along India's West Coast.

After finally arriving at Bombay we set sail for Mesopotamia and a place called *Basra*, leaving Bombay on ***24th October***.

We are all relieved when we set aboard the ship for the final leg of our journey. Again the excitement gives me a rush.

We all get given life jackets! Blimey, is this going to be a rough trip? It was just as a precaution we are told though. Worry was probably written over some of our faces.

The ship takes us up through the Arabian Sea, which does get a little rough as we cross it. It gets quite windy which stirs up the sea.

We travel up towards the Gulf of Oman. (I know this as I hear an Officer say so). I think of A.J. right now and how he would be buzzing if he was here next to me. The Gulf has a narrow part of it, a bit like the Suez, I think, with on one side Arabia and on the right hand side of us Persia. Blimey, I am right up close to Arabia, and will soon be near parts of a country that I have read about in story books as a kid.

The winds drop too a bit, and the journey gets better.

As we get past this narrow part of the Gulf we enter the Persian Gulf. It's strange when you look at the vast countries on either side of us, as one is flat and the other mountainous.

My mind starts to wander a little and I suddenly think of this name *Meso-po-tamia.* I can only say it slowly as I feel I might get myself all tongue-tied. It sounds almost unreal don't you think? As though, like in a fairy tale, it's a made-up name of a country. However it isn't and I am going there right now. Blimey what a turn up for the books and something new to write Mum and Dad about.

We arrive at *Basra* on ***30th October.*** Blimey what a place this is. I've never seen anything like it since arriving in Bombay. I don't know quite what it is but after travelling on the ship and then arriving at a place like this, well, it's a shock to the system is what it is.

There seems to be so many people busying away and the buildings; what can I say about the buildings? They look like they might tumble down at any minute. The windows look funny too. I think, like I said, I've seen similar in India, but perhaps then I didn't quite take them in the first time around.

I don't reckon there to be glass in the windows, but it looks like cloth or something similar. Well, they probably are better off with them like that anyway, as the temperature doesn't get much below 70 degrees, so we've been told.

We all disembark and as the first part of this land is actually marshland, we are to make our way up river on two smaller barges.

With all of us and our kit, plus supplies, we were well packed in as you can imagine.

Did I say small barges just then, because I really ought to say that the barges were actually like steam run paddle-wheel boats, and I enjoyed this experience, although my heart and stomach were having 'butterflies', as Mum would have put it.

Along the river banks there were palm trees growing. Anything or anyone could be just lurking behind one of them trunks I could imagine. I was keeping a watch out for any kind of strange movement anyhow.

We made camp at a small place called *Maqil* for the night. All of us are quite happy to just find a spot and make ourselves comfy enough to sleep, as the journey has been a stress on all of us. Were we going to have to face the enemy soon? Am I going to take part in this war? Although I had been through a lot of training, drilling and suffering with not one but two retched diseases, I still felt there was more to it than this.

These were my thoughts as I lay quiet. I think I fell asleep quickly.

I almost jumped out of my clothes as I was suddenly awoken by the chap next to me, as he jabbed and prodded at me to wake me up quick. We were on the move again.

I rolled over and crawled to my feet, grabbing my heavy kit bag as I went. It was still dark; it was very early in the morning. The ground was soggy. We all fell into some kind of order and off we marched to our next destination. I found it difficult in the beginning as I could hardly see where I was going, only the back of the man in front. As it got lighter it got much easier of course.

It seemed just a flat area really and a wet one too. I was told that the plains here get flooded a lot by the many rivers. All heavy stuff has to be transported on the rivers, so I don't reckon we'll be seeing much of a meal or water for a while.

In Mesopotamia: I am ready for action

We march into *Shaiba* on 1st ***November.*** This was the Battalions Headquarters and here men were continuously being trained before being detached to other posts.

The Camp reminded me a bit of Salisbury Plain, as the Headquarters consisted of lots of tents. I suppose I have been lucky from the start of my journey so far to have been staying in Barracks. This was probably going to be the beginning of a whole different experience for me. More down to earth and 'now we are getting to the nitty-gritty' kind of stuff. This is more like it. Apart from catching malaria fever, I've had it good up until now. Not that I've had anything at all to complain about, but I have felt guilty that I haven't had to experience what Tom did or even what Fred and Jesse might be up against. Letters tell us it's been god awful over there.

There was a bit of a change in the wind direction which brought with it a heavy falling mist; did this mist bring for me and our Company a change? Call me a romantic, if you like, but I had these thoughts with me; I felt an eagerness to learn new things and to progress better in action.

The first thing on our minds was to have a well-needed wash.

What I did notice was the difference in the water here. It was very salty.

We all got an inspection about 4 days later by a Lt. Col. Lock. He had come especially to look at the 'new' draft of men. We all stood in good behaviour and I wondered how important this might be. Anyway, I think we all made a good impression on him. He seemed satisfied.

We got word that there had been heavy fighting here the year before and fortunately for us the Turks had withdrawn after suffering huge losses. The British troops, although taking control here had also suffered losses of life. I guess I was among the luckier men to be in a Battalion that hadn't been sent straight here but had gone to India. Isn't it strange how fate plays a role in our lives?

The following month is spent marching back and forth to various places 'digging in' for the night and marching back again. If we are lucky we might reach a place that has previously been occupied and use their dug-outs where possible.

It's a real hub of activity as other Battalions come and go.

Our Musketry practice is kept up to scratch. Have I told you anything about my rifle?

It's a fine looking weapon, the Lee Enfield Rifle. The Lee stands for the person who invented it, or should I say *her*. Most chaps talk about their rifle as though it was a 'her'; and the Enfield part is for the factory I presume, who made it.

To me it weighs, let me say, about as much as a small sack of potatoes. I am not good with weights, sorry, but that's the best way I can describe the weight of it. It's about 30" long. This I reckon is about right, because I must confess I am handy with my hands and can judge a measurement or two.

We've got 2x5 magazines. That's the packs of the bullets, if you like. Equivalent to 10 rounds of ammunition and I'd like to say at this point that we were continually being told and made aware of *absolutely not* loosing or displacing these magazines at any point during transportation or definitely not whilst in combat. That would be, to my mind, very silly if you did happen to misplace them. Well, you'd be in deep trouble, is what you would be in.

The bullets were .303 calibres, which made it a very fine bullet. Not so fine though if you got one inside of you, I would imagine. Oh no sir, that would not do. I hope it never happens to me either.

And the very best thing of all is that this rifle will make anything up to 30 aimed shots per minute. Imagine that, if you possibly can. That is a lot of bullets and I am not talking about a machine gun here, now am I? This is very impressive indeed if you could manage to fire like this. I cannot, I'm afraid, but I am getting there.

In fact, in the beginning I was all fingers and thumbs, and the rifle got me in quite a nervous state! But I was willing to conquer this and was improving each time.

After a while, I guess I'll think back on my eagerness to learn to shoot this rifle and will not think so much of it. It's not a toy.

It begins to get and feel very serious after a while and it is a very powerful weapon.

It's ***15th November*** and an official concert party is visiting the camp. They put on an amazing performance for us all.

It's good for the mind and soul to have some people singing and making us all laugh, especially at the time when we all are away from normal civilisation, so to speak. I am amazed that this sort of thought goes into the army too. It's great.

It's about a week later, I think, and a different sort of gun arrived at the camp. There is in fact not one, but there are four of these 'Lewis' Guns. These impressive pieces of equipment cause quite a stir.

They are three times the weight of our rifles. Not quite as long, but much wider. They have a kind of flat wheel shaped magazine where you would normally put bullets, which can hold up to 90 rounds and, if needed in action, these could do up to 600 rounds a minute. Blimey, that is unbelievable, I think to myself. Also I should mention that although it's called a 'gun', it looks impossible to hold. You need to lie down to use it!

It was not surprising too that these guns would need special courses of training and instruction. These were guns for a much more advanced or older and wiser soldier. I was not going to be envious of the soldier behind that machine, that's for sure.

Let me stick to my own rifle, thank you very much.

Shall I tell you another impressive picture to see? Well, just imagine being on a practice training, in the middle of nowhere (well that's where we are most of the time, but lucky enough for us our commander in charge knows the map and how to get back to base camp) and suddenly, like out of the blue, or to put it another way, out of the dust, you see a whole load of 'patiala lancers'. Ha, I knew I'd impress you with saying that. What the heck are 'Patiala lancers'? I just know is what you are thinking. Let me make myself clearer to you.

Think of the Arabian knights charging on horseback through the desert... Bingo, that's the lancers in a nutshell. It's the best way of explaining what we saw.

Well, a magnificent sight it was to me, but not quite for our commander at the time of training.

I think he and other officers felt quite harassed by these Arabs. They were friendly, make no mistake. It's not as if we were in any kind of danger. But, well quite frankly, they probably thought... what the heck are these silly soldiers doing out here where there is no battle to be fought. Maybe they didn't 'train' like we did, or perhaps that's just it, they were also training. I don't know, but I do know that it wasn't long before they went and so did we.

I still think of them though. I dreamt that night that I was one of them and I was riding on horseback to battle. I would like to be on horseback. And wearing what they wore too, especially the cloths wrapped on their heads. It made their faces look somehow much bigger and bolder. I wonder what we'd all look like with cloths on our heads. It is much more sensible too when the temperature is so hot and humid. Isn't it strange what you can dream about?

A Visit by the Sheikh of Nejd

It's ***27th November*** and we are all ordered to parade for inspection of the troops by Brigadier General Lock. We are told beforehand that we must clean ourselves up sharp and look our best. We had an important visitor to the camp.

Sure enough, as we stand there to attention, we are inspected by the Brigadier General, but not only for his satisfaction but in honour of the Sheikh of Nejd who stood boldly in front of us with his Arab retainers.

You see I know this because we had been given this information beforehand.

His appearance was of great significance in the world of the Arab politics.

It was said that he proclaimed his loyalty to the British government and worked alongside a certain Captain Shakespear.

He makes a speech about the British policy aimed at uniting with the Arabs to strengthen their leaders.

I thought him a very fine looking man and a very tall Arab.

He was shown our latest equipment. It was paraded in front of him, with much pride by the English soldiers.

Maybe all the training and the Lewis Guns arriving have come at the right time.

He certainly had a good impression of the British Army.

He will, no doubt, be shown more of what the British can accomplish, as we did hear later that he was also shown the railway which was being built to cope with transporting supplies. He would even get to travel across the desert in a motor car! I wish I could have witnessed that spectacle.

You have to realize; at the time of this important visit, not all of us were aware of the 'Arab' that came to see us. Many of us, me included, didn't really care much about politics. We had joined the army for our families, ourselves and for our country.

On ***28th November*** our Company marched and relieved 'A' Company from their post at a place called *Ashar*. This is another area of dust. Have I mentioned how this desert dust gets into your hair and on your skin? As the water is also so precious it's very hard to wash. In fact we don't really wash. You might be lucky enough to feel refreshed for all of four minutes and then you're dusty all over again!

It's December already and I still can't get my head around the fact that it feels so warm. Most of the time the temperature is around the 70 degrees!

Camels, Mules and a Mountain Gun

Today it's the first day of the month and I am off marching to a place called Birjisiyeh. We have to 'dig in' and are here for the day occupying a perimeter camp.

We did pretty much the same a few days later but this time going to Magil. You could say that route marches were, for the most part, our main activity.

The differences in being here in Mesopotamia are also the ways of transport. There are camels used to carry the equipment or even soldiers riding them. I've never seen a camel up close before now. They are very strange creatures and quite comical to watch too. Because of their size and height they can appear really awkward, especially when they have to bend their limbs to lower themselves. You watch them and can't help but chuckle a bit.

Mules are used to pull the water tanks and they look real sorry for themselves. Our water is strictly rationed though as it is precious out here, which we are having some difficulty with.

They use oxen when a red cross wagon is sent out with us.

You'll never believe it but yet another sickness has attacked the Battalion and on ***11th December*** we are relieved by 'C' Company and have to return to Shaiba. They say it's an increase of Beriberi which has occurred and I have it too. This was the first we, in our Battalion, had heard of this disease and I can only describe it as like having a very bad attack of stomach pains followed by diarrhoea, with signs of blood in it. It is most unpleasant. Some chaps have been suffering longer with it.

As this was the case we were all put on "light" duties.

These "light" duties however did not mean that we were only left to make our beds or lie in them. No, it meant that, for example, the running in the morning was made somewhat less strenuous! Most of us were doing our normal duties anyway and less of us were coming down with it. A case of the Beriberi would not allow for a whole battalion to suffer.

These were not my words.

After a special arrival of a medical doctor one day, we were all given extra doses of marmite! It was put in the stews that were made as well as the oxo cubes they already used. We didn't have the vegetables like in India though and the meat was none too special.

Well, even if we'd wanted to complain, it wouldn't have helped the poor cooks trying to do the best with what they had. The marmite just made it tastier.

The Battalion seemed to get back on its feet, and thankfully me too and on 15th ***December*** we carried out a night march and attack.

Morning running was continued as per usual too. Well, I thought to myself, this Battalion has already seen, or had malaria fever and cholera, so a bad attack of the diarrhoea is not going to get the better of us.

On ***19th December*** we had a special training. It was a mighty good sight if I do say so too.

Let me explain; one section of the 21st Mountain Battery, who is part of the British Indian Army, joined us when we paraded for attack practice.

The Mountain Gun was not to be seen at first, but it gets put together by the soldiers themselves.

There must have been at least 4 loads that were carried by mules. They were used for the transportation of the gun and, well I guess they did their bit for the army too.

Anyway my point being, that whilst we were getting ready for practice training, well, this gun appeared all put together looking a grand old sight.

The shells that are put into the nozzle are like giant bullets that look fairly heavy as they're put in each time for firing.

During practice they assisted us in our advance with covering fire and must have used up about 20 rounds of practice ammunition.

I thought it a very impressive show.

But then I thought again, that *this was a practice* and that they go out in real battle with these mules, build the gun right where they stand, and fire away. That's something else too, isn't it?

The Mountain Battery was involved in the war well before we came and they helped defend Egypt from the Turkish aggression. This Mountain Battery was a very important part of the British Indian Army. They were now here in Mesopotamia and Persia to help us finish the war.

I don't doubt that this will get done too. They are really good at what they do.

A couple of days later we were marching to an outpost line for night operations.

A LETTER FROM MY BROTHER FRED

IT'S ***24TH DECEMBER***, AND today we are given a bit of a treat with a kind of sports day which has been arranged for us all. These sports include competitions for bombing and entrenching! Come on now, what else did you expect? Anyhow, we all had a good day.

Christmas day was left to us to do as we wished. It started with us going to a Church Service in the morning, of course. Everybody had letters to open or little packages that had been sent over. I had a few letters myself to open. One letter was from Laura giving me some local gossip and wishing me a Happy Christmas and to keep myself as well as can be expected, considering where I am.

She goes on to say that Amy is struggling to cope because she is worried sick about Arthur, him being so far away in Africa.

When I read this I had no idea about Arthur being in Africa so it got me thinking what he was doing over there.

I also had a letter from my older brother Fred. He is in the Royal Garrison Artillery and he writes that he will be in France soon. He also goes on to let me know that Jesse has had his orders come through and he can't avoid it. He has had to go to Canterbury and is in the Middlesex Regiment. He has written his address on the back of his last page.

Private J. Upshall
3/10 Middlesex Regiment
B Company
Bourne Park Camp
Nr. Canterbury, Kent

I have to put my things to one side after I've read his letter, as I feel suddenly very cold and begin to shake. I think of Tom. He was in France. He died in France. I needed a breath of fresh air. God I bet Mum and Dad are worried terrible. I decide that as soon as I've come to my senses I'll write Fred a letter and wish him well; and especially try and keep as safe as possible.

Then I realise that I also must write a letter to Jesse to wish him well. I got myself a beer before going back to my tent. I didn't drink much beer as I wasn't fond of the taste. It was an Australian type of beer, not that I know much about the stuff, never having drunk it before; but when there is not much else and your mates are having a drink, it's hard not to join in. I think the name of the Beer Company, Tooth & Co., also put me off it a bit. I went back in to finish looking at cards and reading my letters.

A Slight improvement had been made in the cooking department. Maybe because of it being Christmas and all, I am not sure, but some of our food tasted better and it wasn't just me noticing it either. You see, we were suddenly being giving brown bread that tasted different. I liked it though, don't get me wrong; (I asked the cook about it and I was told that the bread was made from Indian flour called Atta).

Mind you I haven't quite made up my mind about our porridge yet. It looks a bit like semolina, but it's not, it is an Indian

Frederick George Upshall, aged 18, Royal Garrison Artillery.

Jesse Upshall, aged 21 3/10 Middlesex Regiment (taken at Bourne Park, Canterbury).

equivalent called *suji*. We only have it served three times in a week anyway, but I do eat it even so. As we are on the subject of food, I'll tell you about another food we eat; it is called *dal* and I suppose is like a pea really. Vegetables as I said before are not to be had and certainly no potatoes, so we have to make do with their substitutes. Most of these food substitutes being sent by the Indian Government and apparently the potatoes were ground down and dried. This was also put into the stews but it still didn't make it quite nice to eat though.

As the sickness of Beriberi was improving, (in fact there were hardly any soldiers affected), they were clamping down on the handling of our water. The local water was not to be used any more. Well that made some sense as until now we've only been using the marsh water, which is bloody awful (excuse me), but it is and there is no other way to describe it.

This idea of getting other water had its down side, as companies were ordered on marching duties to go and fetch water from nearby Maqil.

Not that it was for any company a huge hike, about six miles, is not that big of a deal really. Apparently the water here was also too salty and everything that had to be boiled in it took far too long.

❖ ❖ ❖

1917

After the British defeat at Kut, they appointed a new commander, General Maude. He was given extra reinforcements and equipment and continued for the following 6 months to train and organize his army.

The Ottoman army were getting weaker. On 13th December 1916 General Maude launched his attack and advanced up the Tigris River pushing the Ottoman army out of their fortified positions as he went.

Khalil was concentrating his forces against Maude at Kut but General Maude bypassed the Ottoman forces and switched to another bank of the Tigris attacking them from the rear.

The British had captured Kut and continued to advance up the Tigris River.

Guarding Turkish prisoners at Magil

Troops were detached to train for guard duty at Shaiba Siding and our Company were among those assigned.

We had heard that the British Army had been permitted to build the railway at Basra by the Indian Government. I felt quite an honour to be a part of this, as like Dad, I took a liking to trains and the affect they can have on a country. I mean this railway will help tremendously with shifting the army's supplies from Basra to neighbouring towns. I also can imagine the difference the railway will make to the country as a whole when the war has finished.

I suddenly have a thought: when *will* this war actually be resolved? It has already been, what, three years, and there seems no end in sight. Blimey.

While on duty I noticed how red the sand is in this area and the many palm trees along the river. It looked lovely when the sun was going down. The only thing that spoiled this picture I am describing you are the smells. First of all you could smell the oil from neighbouring Persia as they were in Abadan which was close by. Then you would get the smells from the shore which was not at all like a nice fresh sea smell. I can only think of the smell from dirty clothes, mud and sweat all churned up together with the oil.

As we were returning back to camp, we were *attacked* by 2 squadrons of the Patiala Lancers. Remember, I explained what a sight these chaps were. The sight alone of horses charging towards us with Arabs bearing swords and looking fiercer every minute they get closer. I say attack but in actual fact they were acting it all out. It was another part of our training, so to speak. But hey, at the time, we didn't know this, so of course, we got into position ready to deal with our enemy, aim and fire. Luckily for the Arabs none of us got trigger happy. We knew better by now to await the order to fire. This doesn't, however, stop the fact that your adrenaline digs in and your heart starts thumping away.

On the evening of ***29th January*** there was a bit of a panic in the camp when a fire broke out in the Officers Mess tent. The alarm went off and we all rushed outside and had 'fallen in' ready for orders. By the time men were sent to stamp out the fire, the two tents next to it were alight. We dragged out as much equipment as we could from the three tents and the fires were finally extinguished. Apparently word spread around the camp that the fire had been caused by a Primus Stove.

The sickness of Beriberi among the men was virtually contained. Most important of all, no-one had died here of the disease. Blood tests had been taken of me and others that had had malaria, because we could have been at a higher risk of getting worse.

However there were in fact cases where men had been sent back to India. I'm so glad I wasn't one of them.

In the beginning of ***February*** our Company marched to Magil for guard duty there. We were to guard the wounded prisoners of war. They were all Turkish men and there were a couple hundred of them in all. At least all these prisoners were contained and couldn't *roam* around like the ones I'd seen on the Andaman Islands! These were different as they had been captured by us British. Anyway, they didn't look as though they were even going to attempt to move; just sat mostly in silence and looked worried. I wondered what was going to happen to them and where they were going to go. I would not allow myself to feel sorry for them though, as these men had fought and killed our British soldiers.

On ***14th March*** we returned to Shaiba. At least this time travelling back to Camp, we didn't get attacked or ambushed! I wondered what our next orders would be.

Building a Hut 5 feet under!

In the first week of ***April*** the Battalion had instructions to build huts in readiness for the summer. As the temperature is already up in the 70 degrees, this seemed to us to make a lot of sense. (I can remember how hot the tents on Salisbury Plain would get in the summer). We were all informed of the plan.

Yes, the plan.... I imagined we'd have some wood to work with or something, but no. The huts were to be started below ground; we had to dig down to a depth of 5 feet. Blimey what did someone just say? Excuse me but did he just say 5 feet? Some of us were just a little over 5 feet!

The walls above ground were to be made of sandbags and the roof (would we ever get to the roof? I wondered) would be of matting with a 1 foot layer of earth on the top.

We were to start digging as from today (***3rd April***).

Oh yes you guessed it. The ground was hard. It was very hard. Now I have done my fair share of digging in fields back on the farm, helping my dad, but this ground.....whew.... this was not your usual ground. Having said that, I do remember back in Evercreech we did have a lot of clay in the soil. This reminded me a little like that.

That night one of our chaps, who was a clever one when it came to working out anything mathematical like, suddenly called us all over to his bed and he asked us each to give a guess as to how much ground we would have to dig out of each hole? We looked at each other and really most of us had no real idea, but had a guess anyways. You would never believe it, well perhaps you will, none of us got anywhere near his calculations.

After many guesses and beginning to lose our patience altogether with him, he finally came out with it... 90,000 feet of earth for each hut.

Oh, now you've got to be wrong there we all said, and went back to bed!

The next day, you can guess it. Our mathematician just had to know if he was correct in his assumption, so he asked the officer in charge. "Oh, indeed lad, you are quite correct. That is about the figure I heard mentioned. Well done lad. Brilliant."

Not so brilliant for us, was what I thought.

I wished he'd never given us that kind of information. That's just too much to handle. Blimey.

Progress was slow, as you might appreciate!

We were relieved of our duties on and off for the following days and then we were told we would finally be leaving the camp altogether. What, we're not going to see these huts through?

Yes! We were moving on. Good luck chaps with the digging and all.

Well, can you blame me for feeling just a bit relieved?

On ***17th April*** having packed up all our equipment we left Shaiba for *Nasiriyah*. I knew straight away this was different because of the vast number of ranks with us. I reckon there were over 600 men.

We left camp at 2 p.m. and arrived at Shaiba Siding at 2.45 p.m. There were two trains to take us. The first train left at 6.30 p.m. after being loaded straight away with the baggage, mules, officers and men. By the time the men got on the train, there was only room for about 100 of them. The second train left at 8.30 p.m. with the remainder of the men. I was on the second train.

There wasn't an awful lot to see along the way, apart from desert and palm trees near water. Quite frankly, I soon feel very tired and drift into a half semi-conscious sleep. I try my very best not to fall asleep, but my head just felt so heavy, I couldn't stop myself. My dad used to have this saying; when he slept but not deeply, he would say "I am resting my eyes". That's what I was doing.

We travelled all night and reached *Nasiriyah* on ***18th April*** at 7 a.m. We detrained and marched our way into camp along the banks of the Euphrates.

A TRIP UP RIVER ENDS IN DISASTER

THE NEXT FEW WEEKS were hectic, with new Battalions arriving. In fact during the second week of ***May***, we saw some familiar faces. Men from the Somerset Light Infantry arrived after recovering from their illnesses in India.

There were inspections by the Euphrates Front of all Battalions engaged in practice parades. They also inspected the Battalion bombers; throwing live bombs and dummy ones.

It was during one of our combined attack practices that I would encounter my first actual bit of fighting. Under the orders of a certain Captain and having an appropriate supply of rations for our mission and a sufficient supply of ammunition, we all embarked on our journey in a river boat.

Anyway I am sure that things were a little hectic at one point and there seemed to be some confusion between an angry group of Arabs and Turks and what happened next was that one of the boats got fired upon.

I can certainly say to you that, when something of this nature happens, and you're among some hundred or so men that are all geared up for battle with rifles in their possessions, well, it's only a matter of time before you find yourself firing. What did I fire at? I don't know really. Somewhere in the distance of the village perhaps I thought I got a glimpse of a Turk. Maybe we panicked. I panicked anyway when I saw some of our soldiers got hit, I just felt the need to do something.

However in this whole "affair" there were casualties. In fact some soldiers got killed and a number were wounded. I didn't happen to know any of the unfortunate soldiers killed, but that is not the point. I think we had a close call and it could have gotten out of hand. What am I thinking, of course it got out of hand; soldiers are dead and wounded! I am definitely sure that this incident was not a practice attack.

How did I feel about firing you probably would like to know? I didn't like it I can tell you. In fact I hated every minute of it.

To change the subject – When we all returned to Nasiriyah we were relieved somewhat of heavy practice and I managed to get some spare time during training. Well, of course, we all did. Whilst out and about with some lads taking the local culture in, so to speak; I did have my photo camera with me. You know. Just in case I did happen to come upon something interesting. I did in fact.

My mate nudged me in the side and said a couple of natives were in the distance. Don't know why everybody calls them natives. I regret that I just said that. I take it back. I saw a couple of women approaching in the street. I think they were women. They were covered from head to foot in black cloaks. Well, one on top of their heads and the other over their bodies. They were women I might add as the men did dress differently.

I hadn't seen any like this before. Not so covered like they were. In fact on the Andaman Islands the women there were hardly covered at all. In fact they were practically naked. Talk about extremes.

One of the women was just so completely covered that even her eyes were hardly visible. It's a wonder she could see where she was going! Also one of the women had, perching on top of her head, a water jug. It was literally just balancing on her head. And it didn't fall off either. How clever is that!

I quickly got a hold of my camera. Now some of the people do not like a person, certainly a soldier, taking a picture of them. But I made a sign and pointed to my camera and they didn't seem to mind at all. I almost thought I heard one of them giggle.

Snap. There. My second photograph was taken.

I hadn't been using the camera for a long time, so I think this was the only other time. It felt good. Like a journalist would feel I guess. Now I regret taking any of the women on the Andaman Islands. Although somehow I think Mum would *not* have approved if I had done so.

After taking the photograph I was keen on snapping up some more. So, I decided to take one of a man that was sitting on a mule. Why this, you might ask yourself? Well, we had had a discussion earlier about the fact that we had got the impression that men were here accustomed to riding the mule, as it were, and their women folk would walk behind. We had explained to some of these men, or tried to that is, that we, in the army, would prefer it the other way around. It didn't get anywhere, the discussion that is. Anyhow that's why I wanted this in my collection.

After a while we turned a street and found quite a lot of hustle and bustle. A market day it looked like. Here were many opportunities for my photo camera.

I just couldn't help but stand back and take a shot at all these folk too. I mean, the women. They were quite a sight and not for their fashion either, because they all looked the same as for that.

But because of the loads they seemed to balance on top of their heads. You got to give them their due here, wow, clever is what I'd call it. Damn right clever. And they weren't all women either, but some looked like very young girls.

No men were doing this. Why I ask myself? I wondered if they got neck pain! Well, I don't know do I? Perhaps it's like the equivalent of our mothers carrying the bags of shopping from the local store. I mean the men don't do that back home either do they? There are chores for the women and chores for the men. Yes, that's that, I've answered my own question.

A group of women who were stood talking was a chance for me to get a bit closer for my next photo. I wondered too if they weren't rather hot in those cloaks of theirs. But I guess they're used to it. Mind you, they might not have much on underneath!

The chaps with me were moving on, so I picked up my pace to catch up with them. It wasn't an option to be alone on the street, you could never be too sure if you'd be 'safe' or not. That's what we'd been told. When the chaps rested for a while to take in the scenery, I grabbed the chance again with my camera. These buildings must be good for a shot too, I reckon.

I'd just taken that shot when I turned to see a couple of fine cattle resting with their owners. They really take care of their cattle here too. You could tell. These cattle even had head garments on, just like you'd see back home on a donkey at the seaside.

We headed back to camp, but I took a couple more photos on the way. I was enjoying this side of the army. And who knows what amount of interest they'd cause back home, especially when they get to see these photographs of the strong women.

As I was walking back I saw one of the Red Cross carts in front of me being pulled by a couple of oxen so I stopped to take a picture of that too.

I also took a photograph of the *Euphrates River*, just as a matter of interest. It was, after all, close to our Camp.

Nasiriyah
"I wondered if these women weren't too hot in their cloaks."

More scenes from Nasiriyah... and the bridge over the Euphrates.

Beri-beri, extra doses of Marmite and I see a Mirage

I should mention that we have had to lose Lieutenant Colonel W. C. Cox as he is being invalided back to India and many of us in the Battalion will miss his presence as he was a man with a huge amount of energy.

Lieutenant Colonel N.H. Stone will be replacing him; another fine member of the Battalion and also liked amongst the men.

On the ***21st June*** a 'quinine' parade was ordered for the whole battalion. These quinine parades were, we were told, to carry on as from today and be held twice weekly. Of course, we all realized that the quinine was to help prevent us from getting malaria, and I certainly didn't want to get it again, so we knew this was a good thing. But, having to take it was another matter, and twice in one week! Oh, you want to know how we took it. Well, we had a spoon with a small amount and just gulped it down as quickly as possible. The taste was not pleasant. I can only describe it as being very bitter. It wasn't too pleasant either if you suffered from cracked lips, as most of us did, as it stung something terrible.

The heat was now becoming a big problem. A lot of chaps were coming down with heat stroke and I was feeling the worse for wear also. It was almost like feeling semi-conscious half the time.

Then there were the huts.

If you remember I did groan about us all having to dig out huts in Shaiba for the coming summer. Now, the thing is, here the exact same precautions had been made, and, well quite frankly, if it hadn't been for these huts I do believe some chaps might have died. We all began to realise this as time went on.

There was a method in their madness.

Oh no, the beriberi is on alert again amongst us! Some chaps were so bad that they got sent on to a hospital.

During our parades we were all inspected quite rigorously from top to toe. The one good thing that came from all this, from what I can think of, is that we all had extra helpings of Marmite! We'd had this before but I think I forgot to mention it. I liked Marmite. Always have done, so I didn't mind one bit.

It's good for you, my Mum always used to say. It reminded me of home. Mum, I am eating my Marmite like a good son of yours would do. God bless you Mum. I will stay strong with this I reckon.

I suppose one good thing has come out from this beriberi scare and that is that our route marches have been reduced. We only have to march 10 miles now!

It is so hot at times; I am talking temperatures of around the 100 degrees easily being reached, that we can barely wear just our shirts, our shorts and our putties! It is impossible to do anything mid-day and the ground is virtually an oven which does make it difficult to lie down anywhere, even during the night you can feel the heat on the ground. Many of us are suffering and keeling over with heat stroke. It is even reaching 120 degrees in the shade. I am so glad we have our pith helmets and the cloth or puggaree comes in really useful now as it can shade the neck area.

There is a strange thing that happens when you are out here in the desert too. They call it a *mirage* and what it is really is the way the sun plays tricks with your sight when you look out in front of you and towards the horizon. It happens to us during marching or when we just stop during mid-day. It can be quite serious because you can get the illusion that in front of you appears to be a lake, but it isn't. There have already been some soldiers who, despite shouts of 'come back', have run like mad lunatics towards this illusion and end up collapsing of exhaustion in the process. They are left for the Red Cross wagon to pick them up. I'm scared it might happen to me. I mean this heat is enough to drive anyone crazy and the craving for water is so strong that even the very sight of anything resembling this is tempting.

Sometimes when we get the chance to sit and rest, I'll look across the desert and just find myself staring into it; almost wishing I might catch a glimpse of something interesting. All I see is a distant mist, the effect the heat has when it reflects on the sand, which in its turn can look as if it contains tiny bits of glass.

Arab Pirates along the Euphrates River; I get shot in the knee

On ***23rd July*** the Battalion does suffer a great loss when the Second-in-Command dies of failure to his heart, because of the heat stroke which has been ailing him. We knew him as Lieutenant Colonel Edward Hyde.

It dawns on me that through all these extreme conditions, which I have come across during my time here so far, sudden death can still fall on any one of us. We are all soldiers here to do our bit in this war and, if anything, we can expect to get hurt or be killed in the process and that is something that we all realised from the very beginning of signing up. But to die of something else other than a bullet or a bombshell seems to stun me every time.

On the ***23rd November*** I was amongst a group of maybe 100 or more men who found ourselves being sent on a River Boat called the "T.1"travelling up the Euphrates River with about 500 rounds of rifle ammunition. We also had ten days of food rations as well. I thought that there must be some serious trouble further up river as our boat wasn't the only one. Two boats were alongside us carrying machine guns. I say boats but I am not talking small boats at all, these are serious boats which any villager would find alarming to see approaching them from the river.

The very next day the "T.1" starts leaking. It is so heavily loaded with armour and all of us men; it's of no wonder to me. Then the poor boat runs aground because of something in our way across the river. It turns out that the 'something' in our way is a sandbank. Which I expect has appeared due to the rainfall and the constant flow of the river. Anyhow, the boat had to be dug out of the sandbank before we could move. Blimey, this might be a struggle.

After finally managing to start her up again which seemed to take forever, we started off once more, only to run aground yet again. Oh, and another day has passed since we left. By now I think patience was getting the better of the Captain and we had to transfer ourselves onto the machine gun boats, which meant that we were divided into two.

Apparently the Political Officer in a village called Samawa was in despair and having trouble with the natives. So the Captain must have decided to send an Arab on ahead, which probably wasn't taken mildly as much later on this same Arab was coming back towards us. He'd been stripped of all his clothes and looked as though he'd had quite a bad beating too. Later on the poor Political Officer was seen to be approaching on the right hand side of the bank on horseback. He said he'd been fired upon by large groups of Arabs in the village and also warned the Captain that the village we were about to approach after Al Khidr was armed with pirates who were taking over the boats and robbing them of everything on board. Blimey, Arab pirates along the river seemed to me to conjure up very strange images.

Well, guess what the Captain did? He soon solved that little problem by firing shells at the village as soon as we turned the corner of the river and just blew the place up.

Never mind Arab pirates and us awaiting the signal to fire. No sirree he just opens up his guns and shells the place. Of course a party of men were sent ashore to investigate and after finding stores of various food sources, they shared these out among the friendly Arab victims.

Soon we were approaching Samawa and this was very obvious to all of us on board as lined along the river bank were, what seemed to be, the population of the whole village, there were so many of them. They were calling, well yelling more like and even clapping their hands as we got nearer to them.

This audience gave us a good incentive to ready ourselves as we neared the shoreline.

I was armed and all raring to go when the time was ordered. There wasn't a lot of time to stop and think as we were being fired upon as soon as the troublemakers took sight of us. There was no choice in the matter and I hated, once again to fire but I just had to, to pull through. It was either me fire or get fired at. I was by this time all hot and flustered and fired I don't know how many rounds. There are bullets flying towards me and I just manage to jump out of their way. I stand back up as we are told to move on forward. Bloody hell, something has just hit my knee; but although it stings and hurts like hell, this just gets my temper going and I shoot the son-of-a-bitch right back.

Men were scattered in all directions and the next thing I know is I am being dragged away from the scene by a couple of chaps and am back on the gun boat.

Did I black out or what? I felt dazed and bewildered as I looked around the boat. I don't think that some chaps have survived the incident; in fact they haven't.

By the ***30th November*** we were leaving Samawa at 7 a.m and had arrived safely back at Nasiriyah by about 11 p.m the same day. I wasn't the only casualty that came ashore that evening and I found out the next day that several men had been killed. My knee was not too bad and I had come through again and I felt very lucky.

A Boxing Competition

Some of us are just getting over our attack at Samawa and finally feeling a bit better, when the Beriberi hits right back again. Blimey that damned sickness takes it right back out of you. Whether it happened because some chaps were run down anyway, I am not sure, but those who were took ill by it were sent off to hospital straight away.

The remainder of us get our dose of marmite again during Company Parades.

It's now ***19th December*** and we are experiencing some heavy rain falls. The ground seemed to alter from being quite normal in the morning to changing into a complete mud bath the following day. We find ourselves wading in inches deep mud. Not to mention a large area that was under water.

21st December and the rain has stopped. We are having a Boxing Competition on camp. Not quite for me though, but it was exciting to watch.

While I try and look interested in the boxing, my mind is elsewhere. I wonder if Mum and Dad have got my Xmas card yet. It was not exactly the card I would have liked to send to my parents, but there was a bit of a limit as to choice. I suppose we ought to be grateful we even had a choice. It was quite plain; no pictures of a Christmas scene and no fancy lettering, but it just said on the front:

Xmas 1917
Greetings From
Mesopotamia

I personally wouldn't have written Greetings I don't think. It sounds like we are all 'having-a-great-time-here' and 'wish-you-were-here' kind of ring to it. Which isn't true really and no I certainly wouldn't want them to be here with us, even for a short spell.

Inside the small card though are three rather nice verses, which, I guess says what many a soldier would like to have written if they had thought of it themselves and were poetically minded. I most definitely would have wished I'd made it up.

Inside it said:

'Tis Xmas, '17 A.D. 'Tis Xmas, '17 A.D.
And still we face the foe
And our task is undone,
With that zeal and energy
But ere again '18 (D.V.)

We did three years ago.
The victory we'll have won.
May Xmas, '17 A.D
Bring joys without regret.
Just whisper round this tip from me –
We're not downhearted yet.

I think it just about says it all, don't you? Well, I just hope they will get the card in time for Christmas, but then it is wartime, so you can never be too sure. I bet though when they do find it in the post, they will be very pleased to open it and see that I am thinking of them and have made an effort.

Would you believe it? The boxing competition was so successful that we are in for a second day of it! Okay that's it then, I'm going to darn well join in and get rid of some tension. I'd heard it was just 'what the doctor ordered' according to other chaps.

Actually, even though I'll admit myself, I didn't do too badly out of it. I won the first fight. I put all my anger into that fight too. I just imagined my opponent as being the enemy and guilty of killing my brother Tom, which worked really rather well. But my next opponent was probably even more uptight than me because blimey did he pull some punches. He punched me right in the gut and winded me for what seemed like forever. That was it, I'd had enough. He was too smug about winning the fight and I thought he could have at least said sorry afterwards, but he didn't.

Do you know what? I was glad to be put on line duty for the next day, even with a leaky mud hut.

27th December. It had started to rain heavily again on the ***23rd*** and ***24th*** but then it stopped. The mud was drying. But the roads around the camp were still under about 8 inches of water.

Some mail is handed around to us and I have a letter from Mum which I can't wait to open. Of course she won't have had my Christmas card as yet but that doesn't matter to me. She writes:

Dearest Bill,

I reckon we'm gonna be avin rations brought in soon enough as thers worry that ther might com a shortage of certain ousehold items. The meat as been on the pricey side for my liking so ave been eatin rabbit stew more often these days, but that'l do us no harm. I seen a poster t'other day tellin us all to eat less bread.

Any road yer dad has been busy in the garden making sure we got enough potatoes to last us. Reckon we'l be eaten more a them. Queenie an me been knitten ourselves silly of late, makin socks to send off to soldiers on the front. Ave he got enough of em bill? I'll send some anyroad. They been collectin the socks at the village hall quite regularly. We don't mind doin a bit towards the war.

The village cross has been turned into a war shrine and looks a fine sight 'cordin eye. Names of them that ave already died ave been put on a list by the cross too. Our Tom, god bless is poor soul, is on the list."

Mum goes on to explain that Mabel has 'tied the knot' with her Sherman; the knot was tied on 30th June in Sherman's home town in Orrington in the County of Maine. She had heard that Mabel had been very smitten by Sherman in a previous letter, so this wasn't much of a surprise to them all. Well I'm really happy for her. Yet another one tying the knot.

Letting off Steam

31st December. We are having Athletic Sports. Oh boy.

What should I now try my hand at? Maybe some running will do the trick or no wait a minute, there's a kind of relay race which sounds tempting.

I didn't win any races at the end of the day, but none of this is really about winning or losing. It's letting off steam, which we all badly need to do once in a while. You could tell that this is what it's all about by just looking around and seeing the faces of the soldiers. I mean *all* soldiers too. Not just us Privates, but everyone got involved today of all ranks. I guess you could compare such a day with a New Year's office party. Not that I know what that is like, but hey, I have read many books you know, and newspapers and magazines, where you read about this sort of letting-down-your-hair kind of atmosphere.

I've always wondered why this is necessary. Now I realise why. Someone has to give orders, and there has to be a leader of the pack in order to avoid total chaos in life. I am a soldier now and I finally get it. And do you know what is shocking is the fact that we are not all capable of being a leader. How many of us would even want to be held responsible for certain actions or ways in which certain rules are made? Blimey, I wouldn't want to have that kind of tension to carry around all day and every day on my shoulders, I can tell you. My kit is heavy enough on my shoulders without a burden of young men's lives added to the load.

By early March 1917 the British were on the outskirts of Baghdad. The Baghdad Garrison which was under the direct command of the Governor of Baghdad province Halil Kut (Khalil Pasha) tried to stop the British on the Diyala river.

General Maude out manoeuvred the Ottoman forces. He destroyed an Ottoman Regiment and captured the Ottoman defensive positions. Khalil Pasha was forced to retreat outside of the city.

On 11th March 1917 the British entered the city of Baghdad and were treated as liberators. During the confusions of the retreat by the Ottoman army, large portions (some 15,000) of soldiers were captured. A week later General Maude issued the oft-quoted Proclamation of Baghdad, containing the famous lines....

> *"our armies do not come into your cities and lands as conquerors or enemies, but as liberators".*

Khalil Pasha withdrew his battered army and made his way further up the river to Mosul. He had about 30,000 troops to oppose Maude.

After the capture of Baghdad, Maude stopped his advance. He had been denied further reinforcements and felt his supply lines too long, also the summer conditions made campaigning very difficult.

Unfortunately General Maude died on 18th November 1917 of cholera.

General William Marshall was put in command but he halted operations for the winter.

❖ ❖ ❖

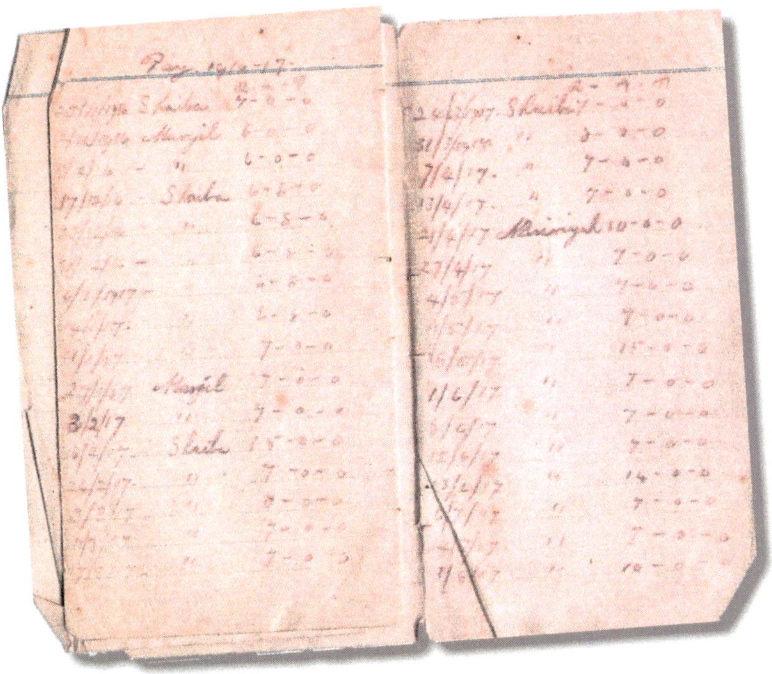

Bill made a note of his pay in his diary.

1918

We lose two chaps on the River Tigris

On ***4th March*** at about midday the Devon's battalion arrive by train. The day is then spent handing over the camp. Another battalion arrives later on in the afternoon and the whole camp is full of soldiers.

The whole of the Battalion Headquarters have changed hands. A and D Company's leave the camp that same evening at 4.00 p.m. and my Company and half of C Company have to wait until the following day. We leave the camp at 6.00 p.m. and our route is to take us towards the city of *Baghdad*.

The whole changeover was quite a spectacle marching out in strength. Over these two days there were well over a thousand men of all ranks and a couple of padres; including around 50 mules and horses. We board a train that same evening and are heading to the Base Camp at Magil, which was near Basra. This might seem a bit strange (well it did to me) but I guess we had to go down to go back up the country or maybe we would be getting new supplies. At the end of the day I just follow my battalion and have learnt not to question the whys and why nots.

On ***6th March*** the train finally arrives around 4 a.m, the Battalion detrains and we are moved to No.1 Camp Magil. I guess there were more than one camp, for it to be called No.1, but I didn't notice any other camps, but then I was really tired after the very long journey.

Some chaps were really going on about the 'damn train journey', but I reckon they should be grateful for there being a train in the

"They looked like double-deck long boats with a canvas roof."

first place, seeing as the Indian Military helped build it for our own behalf.

Obviously we are not staying either because the next day at 1.30 p.m. we are all to embark on a riverboat from a wharf in *Magil*. We were going to travel up river to our next destination. The river we were travelling on was called the Tigris. We were the last group to travel up river as the other Companies had already left the day before.

However it was the ***8th March*** before we finally saw sight of our barge; I guess it had been delayed as there was some cursing going on. I took this delay as an advantage by using my camera to photograph the barges, after all this was quite a sight. They looked like double-deck long boats with a canvas roof.

By the time we were ready to embark on P60 and barges 262 and 506 (their numbers), other ranks had joined us. Blimey are we all getting on board, I wonder. By the time embarkation was completed it was 2 p.m. I just wondered if these barges were safe. With everyone on board, quite frankly they looked like they might cave in with the sheer weight of us all.

It's about 5 a.m. and I was still crouched down in a corner when a voice shouts "just as a matter of interest we are passing Ezra's Tomb". An officer had felt the need to point this out to us all.

I managed to pull myself up onto my feet as we approached a small island. A building with a blue coloured dome was in the middle of the island surrounded by palm trees. I couldn't see a tomb, but then I reckon the building itself was the tomb. As we passed by the mist from the river made the hairs on my arms stand on end, or was it the thought of someone lying inside there. Some of us asked "who the heck was Ezra!" and to this was replied; "Well lads, he was a biblical figure in the bible. A prophet I do believe". You might think, well, not very dignified of us to react, but have I missed the part about it being only about 5 in the morning! He was lucky that some of us were even awake to hear his piece of knowledge!

We arrived at *Amarah* at around 9 p.m. and stay here only a matter of minutes. I think we needed fresh water or something like that.

On ***10th March*** our boat overtook that of the D company and their transport on the PS4. It was 11.15 a.m. We all were wondering what was wrong. Then word had gotten around the barge that a terrible thing had happened. Two chaps were missing.

The two chaps from C Company had fallen overboard. They had been on the upper deck of the PS20. It was about 5 p.m. and they had not been found. A small boat was sent out with a search party on board. I think it was hours that went by. A lifebuoy that had been thrown out was recovered. But no man attached to it and another lifebuoy that had been thrown had suddenly disappeared.

The two had been playing. Well, not playing as such, but I guess they'd been fooling around a bit, as it gets a bit boring on the boat. One of them had lost his balance I guess. This had happened at precisely a point on the boat where there is no rail, only a piece of canvas. He'd fallen through it and as he fell he had grabbed the other chap too and they had fallen together.

The flares that were attached to the lifebuoys would have given them a far better chance of saving themselves, but as they couldn't have grabbed these or seen them, this was not the case.

They were not found. And worse too – we travelled on further. How could they not be found? I wondered. But they were gone. It's like they just vanished. They just didn't surface.

THE MEN ARE NOT FOUND

IT'S 5.30 am and we've arrived at *Kut-el-amara.* We are all ordered off the barge and are sent out on a 1 hour exercise. Which, we all very badly needed of course; not only to get our legs moving but to work off some much needed steam.

We were, all of us, still thinking of the two lost chaps the day before. We had been told that apparently every possible attempt had been made to search for the two of them, even other lads jumping into the river and diving under water to look for them, but the river is not exactly crystal clear and has also a lot of marshland alongside it. They could even have been buried or got sucked into the silt that lies on the riverbed.

It makes me suddenly think of a seaside place in Somerset where, the farther you walk towards the sea (when the tide goes out) the surface is so dangerous it acts like quicksand! Burnham-on-Sea (I've just remembered the name) is the seaside place and I only know about it because there have been accidents reported in the local newspapers and warnings not to walk on it when the tide goes out.

The Tigris can have some swift currents, so I have heard , which is more likely to be the cause of the soldiers' disappearance.

It's still unbelievable though.

By 8.30 a.m. we are all back on the barge and making our way further up the Tigris River. I am not sure which I'd rather be doing, the marching or the standing and sitting on this huge barge.

At the beginning (nearly 4 days ago) it seemed quite a peaceful way of travelling to our next location, but not all of us were aware of how long the journey was going to be and now it seems different. Like the 'lull before the storm' kind of feeling.

I don't think I mentioned either that these huge barges were powered by steam, but I should have because that puts a very different kind of picture in anyone's head as to what they might look like.

When our journey started off, I was alert and keen to look out across this river and watch for anything along the river banks. But now for most of the time there isn't a great deal to see. The odd native village with their huts and palm trees, but as they disappeared very often there was just land and when the hours turn into a day and then another, you just feel very weary. The sounds the power of the steam make and the heat during the day tends to slow you down and in the end I just want to slide down the inside of the barge, sit and rest my eyes.

It's ***12th March*** and we pass Aziziyeh at 6.30 a.m. I must say that the River is getting a little more interesting now actually as it seems to twist its way through the country. As evening draws in we pass Ctesiphon. We are held up here. It's 8.00 p.m.

IT IS SO HOT, WE MARCH IN THE EVENING AND REST BY DAY

ON ***13TH MARCH*** AT 4 a.m. we start off once again. We arrive at about 12 noon at a canal camp, named Khirr Camp, just below Baghdad. We disembark and occupy the camp.

It's ***14th March*** and we all are sent on a route march. I think we marched about 10-11 miles in the direction of Baghdad.

The next day we were back to ordinary parade duties at 4.30 a.m. which took some while to get going as we hadn't had a parade in what seemed like weeks ago.

Then we all got told that orders have come through from headquarters that the battalions will be divided into groups and be heading for *Hillah*. Half of our battalion was therefore split up and we would also be travelling by road as Hillah was across country and away from the river.

We would be leaving the next day, the ***16th***, early in the morning with enough food rations for 4 days and 50 AT carts. We would be relieving one of the battalions of the 53rd Brigade and they would be using the same carts for their return journey.

Our journey didn't quite leave on schedule due to some very naughty ponies. Let me explain - Usually the carts are pulled by mules but we had ponies to pull them. Well, the ponies weren't having any of it. They had all had a rest, I guess, and they were lively things. You should have seen them. They kicked and plunged real frantic like. Some even fell as a result of their behaviour. I bet they knew darn well that they had to perform a duty which they normally wouldn't be doing. I kind of felt sorry for the poor animals. Anyway we got off to a start eventually, when the ponies had given up their fight and had settled down.

By 9.00 a.m we had not only set up, but had moved into our own 160lb tents, as the 56 Brigade Headquarters and the 104th Rifles had not caught up with us. They arrived however at 9.30 a.m.

No, we don't hang around. I guess you might be wondering why we wouldn't have waited for them. But, hey, we weren't to know that they would only be a further half an hour away. Although probably even then our Captain would not have wanted to wait. He was also only thinking of us all. We were all getting hot after our march and needed shelter for a while.

As the temperature was mostly 77 degrees and above, we marched better during the evening time as you can imagine and therefore our arrivals at each stopping place were either early in the morning or late in the evening. We stopped another three more times and I admit to not taking in the exact names of these places.

Whether it is me being drained of energy by the time we halted and my lack of interest by then, I am not sure, but I will just say that Mesopotamia has some of the strangest place names I have ever heard of. Now if it is a small name that sticks in my mind, I will remember it, but quite frankly I am hearing names now which I cannot seem to take in and truthfully to jot them down quickly in my notebook, even if I hear it mentioned, is too stressful as I cannot even begin to fathom how to spell the darned name anyway! What does stick with me is that they either begin with *Al* or *Az*.

On ***19th March*** we arrive at *Al Hillah* and camp at Khirr Canal. These last few days have been so tiring that we were all pleased to hear that we could 'rest' for a few days. I reckon the time spent on the steam barges had taken its toll on some of us, and our energy levels were low. Of course, I speak for myself mostly in saying this, but glancing around I can see it on the faces of other chaps too.

A LETTER FROM FRED: UP TO HIS EARS IN MUD, AND HERE I AM IN 77 DEGREE HEAT

SOME MAIL IS BEING brought around and I am wondering if there is any for me, when two envelopes are thrown in my direction.

One is from Jesse and I start to read it carefully, hoping that it is not going to be bad news. First of all he explains how tough the training has been and how much difficulty he has had coping with it all. Then he tells how he has landed up in the regimental hospital in Canterbury and that for some reason the cause of his illness hasn't been confirmed yet. Whatever the illness is it's causing him to feel very nauseous and he can't seem to keep any food inside of him.

Then he goes on to say that his wife, Emma and their little baby have found a small house to stay in nearby so that they can be close to him.

He tells how most of his regiment have been sent over to France to fight and he hasn't been declared fit enough to join them.

After reading his letter I feel quite pleased for him that his wife and baby are near. Perhaps it wasn't meant to be, I start to think. This mysterious illness might in fact be his saviour in disguise. Of course I feel awful for him that he is very sick but at least he is safe for the time being.

I pick up Fred's letter, take a deep breath and open it. He hasn't been so lucky and tells how he is in France and under the circumstances is quite well. He can't say very much and I get the feeling that it is a lot tougher than he explains. Being a gunner and all it's bound to be horrific. He does say this though:

> *"The Germans are bombarding shells so heavily that the battlefield is a churned up mass of soppy mud. The rain doesn't help. The ground is like porridge, slippery and the going is at a tortoise like pace."*

He wishes that I could send some of our heat over to him, as this would be really welcome right now. His teeth are about the only thing chattering to him and it's getting on his nerves.

I fear for his safety and hope to god he comes through it alright.

A large group of us have been selected to help clear the camp surroundings of all the green foliage, apart from the trees. We have had permission to cut down some of the trees though, as they looked as though they would fall down within time any way and, as our camp was within a matter of feet from these trees, it was feared they might even fall on the tents. Just imagine the news some poor family might get, I was thinking; "son killed by an ancient tree as it fell onto his tent in the middle of the night". I'm just using my imagination again, but that would beat all odds wouldn't it, after what we have all come through up until now.

I take the opportunity of walking around Hillah a little bit and I reckon I may as well make a few pictures while I'm here. I figure it is as good as anything else to occupy my thoughts instead of worrying myself sick about my brothers. Although more than often I do feel awkward with my camera, as I'm not quite sure if someone is going to creep up behind me and snatch it out of my hands or something like that.

I decide on taking my shot with the camera at a young couple who are sat down and between them there is a wicker basket with a baby inside. Then on a street corner I see a couple sat on the street with a kind of homemade canopy propped up to shade them from the heat. These were just simple things and probably very normal to them, but to me they seemed curious scenes.

I decided to end my venture with the camera and leave it at that.

I REALIZE OUR 'HYGIENE RULES' HAVE LONG GONE OUT THE WINDOW

ON ***25TH MAY*** OUR Battalion forms part of a larger column that is to march out of camp. In the column is Major Stone, commanding 1/4 Somerset Light Infantry and there was a column of Patiala Lancers. Also there were 4 red cross wagons and many carts. There were also over a hundred artillery carts of the 56th Brigade Transport. Our march began at 10.00 p.m from Hillah heading for Pinnacle Camp. It would be a distance of about 17 miles and a sight it must look too as we all set off.

We arrive at Pinnacle Camp, Hillah. It was now 4.30 a.m. We pitch camp and rest during the daytime.

At 8.00 p.m the column is on the march once again towards Kala Abasiyeh which would be a distance of 12 miles. We arrive here at 1.00 a.m. Along the way we experience an awful lot of dust. You feel as if it almost creeps all over you and even gets on your face and down your throat. There is hardly any wind, you can't

"A young couple are sat down and between them is a wicker basket with a baby inside.

I see a couple sat on the street with a kind of homemade canopy propped up to shade them from the heat.

even call it a 'wind' if there is one, it's more of a wisp that you notice in an instant and then it's gone. Also the road was very bad.

We are resting for about an hour.

I suddenly get a flash back to the very beginning of my soldier's life and our strict protocol on hygiene. Don't ask me why, well actually I do know why. I suddenly notice some Arabs with rolled up pieces of paper spurting off into the dessert to do their private business and it springs to mind. I find myself having a little chuckle.

What I am about to tell you is a bit awkward, but we have specifically been told to keep one hand for our toilet necessities and the other hand for eating with! What else is a soldier supposed to do in the desert with water so precious? It's not the only time that hygiene hasn't been up to standards either. I am actually wondering if I ought to be sharing this bit of information with you, but there you go – it has been said now hasn't it?

Now we have to cross over the Euphrates River by ferry with the whole column. We start at 2.00 a.m and by 9.00 a.m we have all crossed over safely and commence pitching camp on the right bank of the river. The mules were the only part of the column not over the river yet.

They crossed later on the day though.

On ***27th May*** we are given a rest for the day. I watched a group of men washing their horses in the river. It looked more like a cooling down than a wash though, as the water isn't that clean and the mud on the river bed is so thick that the men struggle to keep upright. The men are cooling off too as most have completely stripped off for this task and I can't say I blame them one bit. The horses seem to like this treat.

Actually shortly after seeing this, most of us strip off too while we've got the chance. I haven't mentioned this before but actually we do get unwelcome guests in our clothes, especially after occupying trenches; I am talking about fleas. Usually we quickly try and take off our clothes shortly before marching to our next destination and kill any we happen upon. I'm afraid it's become part of our routine.

Our company set off again in the evening and we arrive the next day at 8.00 a.m. in *Kufa* and the district of *Nejef.*

On ***29th May*** at 10.00 p.m. a Sergeant and Corporal together with 20 men were sent to reinforce the guard on 11 Arab prisoners. By now most of us had heard of the situation here and I listened to the rumours and the talk that had reached us.

Nejef was a Holy City of the Shiite Mohammedans. These were so called because of their beliefs, or so I was told. It was a walled city which was of great importance to these Arabs. It was here that rebellions had terrorised the inhabitants of the city who were allies with the British and the British had retaliated and besieged the city, cutting off its water supplies.

In response the rebellions had murdered a British Political Officer.

The City was blockaded off until all those implicated in the murder were given up. Our troops were called in to deal with this problem and formed a cordon of military posts around the city, joined up by barbed wire. As it was a holy city there could be no shelling at all. Machine guns were continually fired upon the houses and apart from snipers there wasn't a lot of fighting and the rebels couldn't hold out too long, to the relief of the inhabitants.

The ring leaders were caught and punished.

The thing was there were some Arab prisoners that had to be extensively guarded, so some of us were sent to give a helping hand. In actual fact they were trying to escape. And when you hear why, well I guess who could blame them, well if you were in their shoes, that is.

I am not saying that I would be on their side. They had killed Captain W. M Marshall for heaven's sake.

Not all of them had actually killed him. Some had been among them and were causing riots. They were probably all took prisoner together.

They were due to be executed the next day. Even if they were to escape and be killed, I guess they felt that that would be a better death than a hanging, which was to be their fate.

Eleven Men are hung

In Kufa on ***30th May*** at 5.00 a.m. we have orders to stand to arms on the right bank of the square where the executions are to take place. The 11 men in total were hung.

I am thinking: "Do we really have to be here to witness this? Seeing dead soldiers is one thing, but watching men hang – *blimey*."

Small family groups, I assume, of the victims were mourning their deaths but apart from that no-one else.

The Persians were very relieved at the whole procedure. It was said to be a just cause that they should be hanged; it had to be dealt with and was definitely necessary.

Anyhow here I am with the rest of A and B Company, standing at arms (as it is called) in the square from 5.00 a.m. until about 7.30 a.m. for the whole duration of the execution.

Do I want to be here witnessing this? No. I am thinking. Okay, so they deserve their punishment and all that, but I would rather be not seeing this right now. Some chaps were joking the night before when they heard what was going to happen. You know the sort of thing I'm talking about here. And I am not going to go into any sordid details of what they were saying either. But they were fooling around with a belt around their necks and making strange faces and sticking out their tongues. I laughed, just to prevent them calling me a "party pooper"; you know what I mean I expect.

The thing is, I am thinking, when you're out there in a battle and suddenly have to fire away, you just do it. Without thinking any more of it I guess. But this is different. It is slow and ugh, I would rather look down than across at the scene, is what I am trying to say, that's what I'd rather do.

You might think me a complainer, but that isn't it. Well, okay, I might complain about our conditions, the food and stuff, but I don't really mean it. I mean, come on, there are so many others that have come off worse than me in this war. But, hey, I can't choose where I get put. None of us have much of a choice in this war, do we? We go where we have to and that's that. Yes, now I come to think back, I was excited to be coming to India and 'seeing' the other part of the world. But I did not know what to expect really did I? I might have got plunged into fighting like in France, but I didn't. I get to see this instead. Well this 'sucks' too. And I am sorry for that but there is nothing I can do about it. I just have to grin and bear it, so to speak, like the soldier next to me. But hey, I've got feelings and they're not good right now, that's all.

When we are relieved I feel the urge to smoke a cigarette. I have been trying my hardest to ration myself and only have a smoke when I am in dire need of one. Many chaps have long used up their stash of cigarettes and have invented an alternative. Well, they get hold of some tea leaves and break them up; wrapping this into anything they can get their hands on, to smoke. I try and wait until we get given new packets myself. I've just had a thought; I wonder what Mum will think of me smoking?

I had seen an aeroplane in the early hours of this morning and had thought this seemed a bit unusual, so after standing at arms I asked if anyone knew what that was all about. Well, apparently during the time of the executions, just across from the square a ceremony had taken place to honour the Political Officer for his handling of the town during the rioting which had taken place. It had been a deliberate distraction for the townspeople, which seemed to me to have been a very clever move. No wonder there wasn't a lot of interest in these hangings, excepting the families of the unfortunate men that is.

Nejef and a Holy City

It's a new day and we are on a ferry crossing to the other side of the Euphrates river bank on our way to *Nejef*. Blimey I am so hot that I could just jump into that river; although staring at it makes me feel cooler already. It must be all of 95 degrees out here and already I feel my shirt clinging to my back. I don't know how the natives stick this weather, especially when I think of what most of them dress in as well.

I think about home and how we would always moan about the rain and complain about summer not coming quick enough. Well, right now I can't for the life of me imagine a day without a drop of rain; in fact please rain right now and cool me and my mates off.

When we get to Nejef I shall welcome any form of wash imaginable, even if it has already been used by other chaps (as is usual because of water being so scarce) and they've washed their socks in it!

A few weeks have passed by and I decide to venture out and maybe take a few photographs while I'm here. This will be a place that many of us will remember in years to come because of the riots and of killing a British Governor, not to mention the hangings.

It seems peaceful now which is what anyone would expect a Holy City to be. Maybe we are spending some time here to help get the City back on its feet again.

I don't think I've mentioned the 50ft wall that surrounds the city. I've seen castles with great walls around them in picture books, but this is quite something else. There isn't a castle here at all. But the city is quite large and about in the middle there is a dome which catches the sun as it is golden in colour. I try to take a photograph of this in the background.

I think I've got this retched beriberi again as I don't feel at all well and I am so darned thirsty I can hardly spit. I wish I could drink loads and loads but I can't because I also feel quite nauseous. Until now I've tried to keep it to myself and carry on as normal,

A 50 foot wall surrounds the city of Nejef.

The place where 11 men were hanged.

The entrance to the city of Nejef.

but it's gone beyond that point now and I'm sent to see the medical team. I am not the only chap either with a problem and we blame it on ourselves washing in the dirty river.

Blimey now they reckon I've got cholera. What am I supposed to do now?

They decide to send me to Kufa Rest House on ***25th September***. I still hope they don't send me home though as I want to stay until the end with my battalion. If I was badly shot up or wounded it would be different but like this, no not if I can help it.

I get these darned awful cramps in my body and it causes me to roll up like a baby.

It's just as well I don't have a mirror on me as the skin on my hands and feet is practically shrivelling up like dried plums.

After about three whole days, my nausea stops and I get given plenty of rice to eat. The marmite is still on the menu though so this helps just a little as rice on its own is not at all tasty I can assure you. It seems to be doing the trick though as by the end of the week I feel almost as right as rain again.

It's strange too how illness can affect your taste buds. For the first time in ages I seem to be getting used to this tea without milk. I am actually thankful to be sipping it right now.

By the beginning of October I'm back with the battalion again. The Battalions are to be moving towards Baghdad. One company will be travelling by road with the transport and the other by way of the river.

Guess which Battalion was travelling by road? Yes, B Company. Blimey I hope we are not marching all the way to Baghdad. It might be October, but the temperature is still hotter than most English summers.

A TRAIN CALLED ELEPHANTA AND I PASS THROUGH BABYLON

IT TAKES US ONE and a half days to travel about seven miles, but then we still can only travel in the evening and until the early morning.

By ***5th October*** we march into a place called Kifl, the time was 10.00 a.m. and we camp down near a resources wharf along the left side of a river bank.

It's ***9th October*** and we are all to be moved onwards to *Tekrit.*

Orders were read out that there would be two trains leaving *Hillah* tomorrow. The first train would leave at 9.15 p.m. loaded with all the baggage and transport plus two platoons, and they have to pick up tents at Baghdad. The second train with the remainder of the Battalion leaving at 11.30 p.m. will go straight to *Tekrit.* This was the train that I would travel on.

A large number of men (around 70 from A and D Companies) had to stay behind at *Hillah* in isolation, due to an outbreak of smallpox. Thank god I wasn't one of them. I don't think I can handle any other forms of sickness, thank you very much.

The train was pulled by an engine with quite a memorable name: 'Elephanta'. Anyway this train will be taking us along a fairly new part of rail and this rail was only a narrow gauge.

We crossed part of the ancient city of Babylon and, in actual fact; I think we even went through some walls of the ancient city. Imagine it, being so close to a place like Babylon? This is a holy place that you only read about in the big old bible during Sunday school, apart from the natives who live here that is, and now I am travelling right past it. Blimey, it's a pity I can't stop the train and have a good look, I'm thinking. But then again under these circumstances it's best I put that idea to the back of my brain and not think about it, still it would have been great though, don't you think? I certainly will have to mention this train journey to Dad when I get back home, seeing as he has worked on the railway and all.

He might even be reading something in the local newspapers about how the British are helping to build the railway lines here in Mesopotamia.

It has just occurred to me that the name of this train, Elephanta, is actually a very good name when you think about it. An elephant is a very strong and powerful animal and if it were to charge at anything it would cause quite a panic. A train is a very strong and powerful machine and nothing would stand in its way when it's racing along the tracks. It's a perfect name for a train!

We arrive at *Tekrit* on ***11th October*** at about 2.30 p.m. and are told that we have to bivouac at the railhead overnight. There must be over 500 of us altogether. I don't reckon anyone was particularly bothered where we stayed to be honest as long as we got some rest.

The country this far north seems to be barren and the ground beneath our feet isn't really like sand anymore but a fine dust. This dust got the better of us on several occasions. Somehow or another it manages to creep into everything. The dust is even getting into our bags and our guns have to be well protected as best we can and we find we have to keep the leather oiled in order to protect that too.

We all march onwards and make our way towards a camp about 8 miles north of *Tekrit*.

After a short overnight rest we march on again and arrive at another camp which must have been around a similar distance to the previous one. The ground here was quite stony underfoot and digging trenches has proved very difficult indeed.

We move on once again, as by now it had occurred to all of us that we were driving the Turkish army further and further northwards and are part of the force giving the Turks the final push.

It seemed to be working too. We move again a further 10 miles on ***29th October*** and we were by now about 20 miles North of Tekrit.

I reckon the Turks were probably outnumbered by us British as the only force that was used were the Lewis Guns, which we constantly heard in the distance.

On ***6th November*** we were joined by over 50 men who said that they had been in hospital, recovering from influenza!

Blimey I forgot to mention that what do you reckon our Battalion has been doing now that the Turks have, it seems, disappeared altogether? Well, we are helping out with the further development of the railway line. I am not kidding either. How is that for coincidence, if ever there was any of the like? Wait until Dad gets to hear about this. Do you know it's just given me a thought? I must write a letter to him when I get a moment and explain all about it, he'll like that.

It seems that now our Battalion is relieved of work on the Baghdad Railway. Oh well I guess I spoke too soon, at least I can say I did help for a short while though can't I?

Now we have to march back to Tekrit - it's ***8th November*** and what do you think, it's raining! I don't normally mind the rain, but now it's raining very hard. It has got a bit better towards this afternoon though, which is a relief, or we might have not needed to march but could have swum!

It's the day after and we have been allowed a day of rest. Actually we have to wait for a train to become available. The trains were at the moment being used to take prisoners and captured animals to Baghdad. I am not a bit bothered as I don't reckon I could have marched much farther.

THE WAR HAS ENDED

IT'S ***11TH NOVEMBER*** AND we all get this wonderful news that the War has finally ended. We hear that there are celebrations all over the place. We jump up in the air; throw up our helmets and anything else we can get our hands on. *Blimey* I just feel so relieved that I want to scream it out, dance and skip about all at the same time!

I feel relief for all of us and for all the chaps in France and wherever else they might be. I feel relief and hope for my brothers and please God let them still be safe today. This means we shall all get to go home very soon and live and get on with our normal lives again.

Actually I get quite emotional and am not sure whether I am laughing right now or crying. I must be still weak from that last illness.

It's ***13th November*** and I am lucky to be among about fifty of us in B Company who get the chance to escort some Turkish prisoners to Baghdad. We have Captain Baines in charge of us all; lucky for him. The prisoners are no trouble at all; in fact we hardly would know they are on the train, they are so very quiet. I suppose they are wondering what will happen to them and actually I find myself also wondering what will happen to them.

It occurs to me that Baghdad and for that matter all the other places we now travel to should be safe now.

I want to take a picture of something here in Baghdad while I'm here and I just about manage to take one before being hurried up by the chaps around me. Oh well perhaps somebody else has taken some of the city and I shall get a chance later on to look at them.

We have only been here a day when we have to leave Baghdad and cross by barge to *Hanaidi Camp*, which we reach in the afternoon of ***15th November*** and we are told that we shall be staying here for a few days; which is a relief for us all.

In the days following other Battalions keep arriving and the Camp begins to fill up. There is good humour all around and we seize this opportunity to smarten ourselves up a bit too. We manage to have our hair cut, which does do us all good, and pose for photographs as well.

Street scene in Bagdad.

At Hanaidi Camp. (I'm the one with the cross.)

I get a kind fellow to take over my camera and get me into a picture for a change. He says he'll take a before the haircut and after the haircut photograph. In the latter we make a proper job of it by posing in a mannerly fashion.

I couldn't help it but myself and some other chaps went a bit mad, when we wrapped ourselves in blankets, grabbed anything else we could lay our hands on, made headgear and posed as Arabs with a board in front saying *No.8 Platoon*. I then had our photographs taken as a statement for later of how relaxed we all, as soldiers, were finally becoming. Plus the fact of the matter was that we all had a good old laugh out of it in the process!

On ***22nd November*** we leave Hanaidi on route to *Ruz*. We board a train for this journey and the next day, the ***23rd November,*** we arrive at Ruz and make camp.

The amount of soldiers that were in this camp was up in the hundreds and possibly nearly reaching a thousand.

On our arrival the Battalion came under the orders of the 14th Division. I'm not quite sure how this worked but it seemed that some soldiers were travelling to other locations; which also seemed a bit odd to me as I reckoned now the war has ended, we should all be travelling in one direction only. Back the way we came here and off towards home. Well, who am I to suppose such a thought. As long as I stick with the soldiers I know then nothing could go wrong.

Oh and which battalion got furthers orders to march with most of the 'dump' to Mirjana do you wonder? Yep, you guessed right; ha-ha, our battalion. But do you know? I don't care anymore and none of the other chaps are too bothered about it either. I reckon if we didn't have so much to carry, we could have run there. We are all gradually going home soon and not the slightest thing can bother us. Well, except for the stupid Beriberi or one of those other retched diseases that is.

Hanaidi Camp. We pose for a proper photo, all looking and feeling much tidier after our haircuts. I'm in the back row, 2nd from left.

We wrapped ourselves in blankets, made headgear and posed as Arabs with a board in front saying 'No.8 Platoon'. I'm in the middle.

We leave Ruz on ***1st December*** on our route march to *Mirjana* and arrive there that same night. I reckon the distance was about 17 miles.

We are to spend our time here constructing the Camp in preparation for the winter. The Camp itself is called the Mirjana Kizibabat Camp. And what a mouthful that is to say too, mind you I can only guess at the spelling.

Whilst I have some time to myself and write a couple of things down, my eyes notice one of my addresses that I had written inside my book. It was an address I had jotted down on the ship before leaving at Bombay. As some of the soldiers had orders to travel in a different direction at the time, I had noted down the name and number of a buddy of mine and he had done the same. In the very beginning we had heard a little from one another but then nothing. I realise now that I am in the exact camp he must have been in about 3 years earlier. I wonder what happened to him.

Awaiting Demobilization

I was happy when a small number of men were allocated in the making of a Brigade Garden at the camp and I was to be one of these men. It was now obvious that we were going to be staying here for several months and I was glad to be taking part in this project. Actually although it's December, the weather here couldn't be better for a garden this time of year. It's still around 30 degrees and it rains more too. So if you wanted anything to grow in this country, this would be as good a time as any to start it up. I also loved to be gardening too.

You might think to yourselves, that now we won't have to march for a while, but you'd be wrong.

We still had our route marches that were done on a weekly basis. Also we did night operations. Well, excepting the Christmas week, we did not have to do any then.

We also had to do battalion attack practices and lots of drilling, but apart from that, no other training went on.

We all got T.A.B. inoculations. You see, we have been told that we are all awaiting demobilization, and to make our time here less tedious we have to be kept busy.

The British resumed their offensive in the latter part of February 1918, capturing Hit and Khan al Baghdadi in March and Kifri in April.

For the remainder of 1918 the British had to move troops on to the Sinai and Palestine Campaign in support of the Battle of Megiddo.

General Marshall moved some of the forces east in support of General Lionel Dunsterville's operations in Persia during the summer of 1918. His very powerful army was "astonishingly inactive, not only in the hot season but through most of the cold".

The fight in Mesopotamia was not needed anymore.

Armistice conditions between the Allies and the Ottoman Empire began negotiations in the beginning of October.

General Marshall followed instructions from the War Office to the following: "that every effort was to be made to score as heavily as possible on the Tigris before the whistle blew" and subsequently went on the defensive one final time.

General Alexander Cobbe commanded a British force from Baghdad on 23rd October 1918. Within two days his force covered 120 kilometres and reached the Little Zab River. He expected to meet and engage the Ottoman Sixth Army which was operating under Ismail Hakki Bey. He fought at the Battle of Sharqat and captured almost the entire Ottoman force.

On the 30th October 1918 the Armistice of Mudros was signed and both parties accepted their current positions. General Marshall accepted the surrender of Khalil Pasha and the Ottoman Sixth Army on the same day.

General Cobbe however didn't hold his position as the Armistice required and despite Turkish protests he advanced on Mosul. The

British troops marched without opposition into Mosul on 14th November 1918.

The ownership of Mosul Province and its rich oil fields became an international issue.

The war in Mesopotamia was over on 14th November 1918. This was 15 days after Armistice and one day after occupation of Istanbul.

❖ ❖ ❖

Kizibabat. We stay here awaiting our demobilization.

1919

We finally get word of our Demobilization

A new year has come again and some days have seen enormous rainfall and, in fact, leave much of the surrounding countryside under water.

There are even schools being set up to learn for example Urdu, Arabic, shorthand and even building.

A number of us looked in on these classes, but after a while they had to stop. The school masters that were holding these classes were among some of the first to be demobilized!

Oh you wonder if I had a go at some Urdu don't you. Well, as a matter of fact I did manage to get my head around a couple of words:

Thank you = *Shukria*, Yes = *Jee haan* and No = *Jee nahin*.

Also I liked the sound of this word:

Great = *Zabardast*

I thought I ought to learn this word as well:

Goodbye = *Khuda hafiz*.

But when we heard that Urdu has around 52 letters to its alphabet, well blimey did that sound like a nightmare. I have to stop and think of just our 26 letters let alone twice the amount!

No, I am quite happy with the few words I have learnt and I jolly well hope I can remember them. I figure if I practice on the chaps and hum them to myself, I might just manage it. I've never been one for having too much of a memory, so it'll please me no end if I can still remember them when I get home.

Most of our afternoons have been spent with games or playing football. I guess that you can imagine which one of the two possibilities was the most popular? You guessed right - football. Now football was a bit down my street to and I was glad to join in.

The Officers in charge are, however, doing a very good job of keeping the Battalion occupied, whilst we all await our turns for demobilization.

We are also kept occupied with regular route marches and some range duty too, so it is not all fun and games.

On ***11th January*** we have a very heavy rainfall. It has kept up all day. By now much of the countryside is under water.

It's another day and still raining.

There is a lot of activity around the camp as over 200 men are to be the next to demobilize. They have to be prepared and ready to go as soon as orders are known. As you can imagine, for these chaps the tension is high.

A week has almost gone by and the men have still not had orders yet that they can leave. By now they are a bit uptight. I can't blame them though.

The rain has begun to calm down by the end of the week, but by the ***18th*** we're once again experiencing very heavy rain.

On ***24th January*** the chaps who had been waiting to leave have finally had confirmation. Blimey, fancy having to wait all that time. I wonder how many times they packed and unpacked or, I suppose, didn't pack and had to rush it all at the last minute. I reckon that's what I'll do if we have to wait.

There are so many different groups here waiting and it's all done in fairness and everyone involved appreciates this.

On ***3rd February*** it's our turn. Our Battalion gets ready for demobilisation. Blimey that word sounds quite exciting really, in a strange way, and I'm sure there has been a certain system in doing all of this. We leave *Mirjana* and are off to the base camp arriving there at night and I had a good night's rest here before leaving the next day.

We are now on our way towards *Kut*. By now the heat has already risen to probably over 70 degrees or it might even be higher. All I know is it's getting hotter and marching in this weather is not easy when you've got sand beneath your feet. I think I might have seen enough sand these last couple of months, or is it years, to last me a fair while and I might even give a trip to the beach a miss when I'm back home too.

When we are approaching the small town of Kut, I notice the mud-houses dotted here and there. They seem to be almost in a state of ruin and I'm sure they are deserted. I wonder if new inhabitants will make use of them once more, now the country will be safe again.

We've been travelling all night and now we've arrived here before mid-day, I am hoping we'll be catching a rest before our next march.

As we march onward once again towards our next destination, *Amara*, I can't help but wonder if we've been walking on the very same ground as our earliest ancestors. You know, from the bible, like Abraham and all those important people that you get to read about in church or at home. Not that we, in our family, grew up with the bible on the table or anything like that. I mean, we do have a bible in the house but very seldom do we actually pick it up and read it. Maybe I'll just do that one day when I'm back home resting. Just to be curious, I'm thinking, to see if it mentions such places as I have travelled. Babylon is one for certain that's in there, because I remember it. Sad it is too; that these places where history is made of, have now been almost dissolved into the desert, or become part of it and all that might remain is a mound and a ruin.

I've just had a thought, me thinking all this has made me remember that we have the exact same sad remains of history too. Like Stonehenge, where I also marched beside and the grassy covered mounds around Salisbury Plain. I hadn't thought of them like this, but now they come to mind. It's funny how a mind can wander when marching along this desert!

Of all the places we have to stay for more than a week, it turns out to be Amara. I can't explain the feeling I felt and other chaps too whilst we were there. Around about the same period two years earlier this had been a place of battle and it didn't look much better now. Of course, there was now no fighting or shots to be heard or cries of the wounded or anything like that, but the graves were here of men that had died and fell onto this ground. I also know that men didn't only die from a fired shot either, but from the conditions here like the heavy rainfall and the cold feeling when your clothes cling to your body and you shiver. Well, anyway, blimey, when we set off again was I glad to get away.

It's ***20th February*** and we've reached *Magil* and I am happier to be marching into this camp at *Makina*. For one thing, this was near enough where we started off 2 years ago. Blimey has it been that long ago? Look at us all now. We've changed somewhat in those years. Do we look a slightly different colour too? I can't quite make up my mind if this has been due to some lack in keeping ourselves clean, or it could be due to the sun giving us all a tanning. We are here for a week or two, or so we've heard, waiting for the next ship to arrive. It won't be long now before we are back on 'home ground'.

Aboard the H.T. Elephanta and through the Persian Gulf

THE TIME FINALLY COMES to leave the 'rest' camp on the ***4th March*** and embark our ship. I notice the name that seems to have been written onto the side of the ship: *H.T. Elephanta*. That rings a bell. Where have I heard that name before? I can't think for the minute, but it'll come to me some time or another.

We are all in good humour once we've embarked this large ship. It's a buzz of excitement on board and quite the contrast, of course, from our first experience reaching these new shores. The first thing I manage to do is to get hold of four pancakes! Yes, I made a bee-line for the kitchen I'm afraid. I just reckoned the food on board was going to be so much better than what we've been used to. They were the best I've ever tasted too!

Off we go back down through the Persian Gulf. I'm saying this now as it will be the last time I can. It's not likely that I'll get to travel this far ever again, so each day I am on board I take it all in.

It's not very wide and I can see the land on both sides. As the ship travels down the Gulf, on the left is Persia and on the right hand side is Arabia. I suddenly catch a sight of a pair of dolphins just away from the ship. I shall remember this always; and I don't just mean the dolphins, but all of it.

Blimey, I've just remembered where I've seen the name of the ship before. It was on the train journey towards Tekrit and I had realised at the time what a great name Elephanta was for a train. I thought it sounded familiar, didn't I? I reckon though it's a more fitting name for a train than a ship. However I do like this ship.

We travel through the narrow part of the Gulf, called the straight of Ormus, and I am looking out across at spectacular high mountains. In fact on both sides there are mountains. The ones near to the shore look chalky and white. The scenery is so amazing to watch that it practically takes my breath away! Again I can't remember feeling this on my journey nearly 2 years ago, but then I guess I feel different now that the war is over. Not that we still don't feel a bit cautious wondering what might be lurking out there, because I do still feel weary that eyes might be watching us. I guess it will take some getting used to after all this time.

We soon reach the open waters of the Arabian Sea and our destination is Bombay. When I think back to 4 years ago when I first set foot on Indian soil it seems like a lifetime away now. I remember I felt anxious and scared at what I might see and have to do. Now I don't know what I feel.

I probably won't see India anyway, as I would imagine we are put on a different ship and sent on our way. But I won't forget India at all.

We arrive at Bombay on ***9th March*** but we can't move away from the docks as, just as I thought, we have to be transhipped onto the S.S. *Tahiti*. The buzz of soldiers talking and goods being shifted from one place to another is a very hectic scene indeed and, of course, the atmosphere is not of the doom and gloom that it once was, but one of anticipation of getting just that little bit closer to returning home.

I can't help but think of A.J. and other chaps like him who we have had to leave behind here. I wish that it could be possible to pay my respects to him but I can't remember where he was buried. I feel dreadful and ashamed that I can't recall the place and find myself sitting down on a crate whilst I rack my brain to pieces. We hadn't been in India that long really when I think back and we were all struggling with the heat and the damn mosquitoes. Was it Calicut where we were or was it the place before that?

"Come along Bill, quit your daydreaming lad and get back with your Battalion, or you'll be putting yourself on the wrong ship if you don't stay alert my boy". Somebody pats me on the back so hard I nearly fly off that crate.

I hate it when Officers call us 'my boy' like that. I *am not* a 'boy' any more, why can't they see that none of us are. We've grown up and got older.

It's about three in the afternoon when we board our next ship. She's not so grand looking as the Elephanta, but probably more fitting for us lot travelling back towards the Suez Canal.

The heat is increasing now so it will be more comfortable travelling by sea. As long as I'm not seasick, I hope to enjoy this journey. If the sea is not too choppy, I reckon I shall cope better this time around. Blimey my stomach has had to put up with a lot worse over the years so this should be a piece of cake now I reckon. I wonder if we'll see some whales on our way.

I decide to eat modestly and take my time over the next week or however long our journey takes, as I want to spend as much time on the deck of this ship as possible and take as many pictures as I can. When I say 'take as many pictures', I don't actually mean with my camera. The fact that first of all I have no film left and secondly we are moving and I am sure that if I did still have some film, I would bosh them up anyway! No, I mean I shall take a 'mental' picture of the sea and the distant mountains along the way; and any wildlife will be an extra bonus.

We arrive at Port Suez on ***19th March*** and disembark the same day. This is a welcome surprise to us all, as we hadn't made a single stop back in 1915 as I recall.

We are making our way towards a camp a few miles from Port Suez. It was near the canal, but quite frankly I didn't sit and watch any ships going past as I, and most other chaps, took this opportunity to get some much needed sleep. My sleep since leaving Magil had been at a very minimum and now was as good a time as any to catch up.

Within two days we get word that we are going to be travelling by train to Port Said. *Blimey,* I thought, they do want to move us all on quickly. But hey, I was going to be riding on an Egyptian Railway Line; what a surprise this was.

We leave in the morning and by the afternoon had reached our destination. Except for sand and some hilly dunes and the sight of the canal, I'm afraid there was not much else to enjoy. Also, to be honest with you, despite my catch-up-on-my-sleep time, I actually dozed off again!

As we await our next ship to arrive, we have more time to rest ourselves. This time is spent mostly at our rest camp being 'checked out' medically and we have the chance to give our clothes a well-earned disinfected wash.

I also make some time to wander around parts of Port Said while the opportunity arises. It's very nice here and the buildings along the main street are colourful to the eye. Most have pink walls and brown wooden balconies along the whole of the building. Their roofs have red tiles and there are plenty of windows to let in the air, but all of them have shutters to keep out the heat. Most of the small shops have striped canopies to shelter the passers-by as they stop to look at the goods displayed. In front of the buildings and stretching as far as the eye can see, is a short fence separating the front street from the canal edge. Sections of the canal have little moored-up wooden boats along them. They remind me of home and the seaside villages we would now and then make our way to during the summer holidays, if we were lucky.

The buildings are similar to the ones I remember seeing at Wellington where I also had the chance to rest after catching malaria. I feel a shiver down my spine as I remember the fever and am glad that I shan't be catching that again. Actually I'm grateful I survived the fever; many fellow soldiers didn't get so lucky, and there I go seeing A.J. in my mind again.

To the Port of Marseilles and by train through France

It's a grand old sight watching the large ships dock at *Port Said,* I can tell you. Our ship is called the S.S. *Canberra* and what a fine ship she is too. Her large steam funnel is right in the middle and there are tall masts towards the front and rear of her.

We get to embark on ***27th March*** and by the time we are all on board and she is ready for her voyage another day has passed by. But we don't want to worry about that as we are on our next part of our journey towards home and family.

I am feeling very anxious by now and I stay on deck as long as possible. We seem to travel along the coast of Egypt first of all and only start to alter our course when we approach the coast of Libya. I can tell you this as I take note of what is being said around me. My ears prick up, which on many a time I have been teased about, as they do stick out rather a lot; well, all the better for me I reckon.

I want to breathe in as much of this Mediterranean Sea as I possibly can and the warmth of the sun is so good, just what the 'Doctor ordered', as Mum would say.

We still have to do some drilling on board the ship first thing in the morning but we are so enthusiastic about getting on deck each day that we even start surprising ourselves.

We soon reach the coast line of Sicily. It's a very clear sunny day and I can see wild and rugged mountains as I look out across the sea to the land ahead. Thinking about land ahead, reminds me again of my younger self reading picture books of pirates attacking ships that cross their paths and reaching far away islands and looking for treasures. I wonder what treasures there are on that island over there?

We pass along another island as the ship seems to be turning towards the right a bit. I had my ears pricked up again this morning at breakfast time and have heard that we are not heading in the same direction as our first journey across these waters took us. Well, blimey, I'm not complaining about that as I recall we all had a terrible journey once we had set out from Southampton and everybody had been seasick. Perhaps that's why we are taking a different route home; they don't want us all to look any worse than we might already!

This next island is not unlike the name of those fish, sardines; as it's called Sardinia. I must have been thinking out loud as I am told that they are actually caught around these waters. Well, that explains the name then doesn't it. I can't remember ever eating them myself though, but I do recall we could often buy them in India along with other extra articles. As I think back, I did buy sausages and eggs once. An Officer reckons sardines are on the menu for tonight! Is he pulling my leg?

This island looks hilly as well as rocky.

I am watching a pair of dolphins as they swim along the ship. They can jump out of the water and they almost look as though they are smiling at me. It's wonderful to watch them swim. They swim pretty quickly too, at least as fast as our ship anyway. I must say that the water looks so inviting, well, I could practically jump in it myself. Of course I won't though, as it would cause havoc among the rest of the chaps. I can just imagine it – 'man overboard' and all. Blimey, what am I thinking? I suddenly get a flashback to our trip on the barges and the two men being lost on the Tigris River when they fell overboard. Am I always going to get flashbacks?

Corsica is apparently the next island we pass by and it seems much similar to the other islands, apart from some sections of cliffs that have a reddish colour to them. It's really vivid and no, it's not the sunset turning them red either, as the sun isn't setting yet. On some of the high rocky parts there also appears to be houses on top of them. Blimey, that must have took some doing to build them like that, and dangerous by the looks of it. Fancy that, living right on top of a cliff. It wouldn't be somewhere I'd like to live, no sirrée, not the safest of places to put your house, although I bet they got a pretty good view across the sea.

Our ship arrives in the *Port of Marseilles, France* on the ***2nd April.*** We spend a couple of days in Marseilles before setting off on a train through France. The carriages seem to be all doors as we all step aboard this very strong looking steam train.

We don't seem to have travelled very far before we stop off at a place called *Arras* (or that's what it sounds like) for a wash.

Back on board we travel through steep hills with viaducts not unlike those at home. The scenery is a pleasant change from the desert lands I've been accustomed to these last few years. The green hills and fields around make me feel closer to my homeland. I can't help it, but I find myself falling in and out of sleep very easily, which I feel quite annoyed about as I would rather take the surroundings outside the train into my mind.

We stop at Malisherbes for another wash. They certainly want to keep us looking clean, I think to myself. But still it's nice to step out of the train again and stretch the legs, that have, I admit become quite stiff with all this sitting about.

Back on the train again we travel still northwards. We have left the higher hills behind us and many of the men, including myself, have gone quiet now. We are coming in to land which has been affected by the long battle of the war.

Before long we have stopped again at a place called *Juvisy* and we are told that we will be here for about two and a half hours.

For a place on the outskirts of Paris, it seems pleasant enough but I don't feel at all like going for a walk. All I seem to be thinking in my mind is I wonder how far Ypres is from here, where my brother Tom died in action. I don't bother asking anyone though; what would be the point? It's not only my brother Tom who has lost his life here in France, but so many other brothers, sons and fathers too. I wonder if Fred is back home yet and Jesse, how has he been? I can't explain how relieved I am when we are told that we can board the train for our last leg of the journey.

I close my eyes during this last part as I feel quite drained in my thoughts and any glimpses of battlefields that there might possibly be, I do not want to see them at all.

We cheer as we arrive in Southampton

On the ***7th April*** we arrive at *Le Havre* and march into a camp about three miles from the town. We leave the very next day and make our way back to the harbour and I lifted my feet off of French soil and stepped right on to the U.S.S. *Yale*.

This ship was a little different to the others I'd been travelling on, in that it looked like a cargo ship. It had almost straight sides to it as a result and looked a real stocky old girl. She had two steam funnels and two large masts fore and back. Not that it mattered to me what kind of ship we would be getting home on;

I probably would have got on anything small or big as long as it took me back home. Anyhow being so stocky might be of an advantage against the choppy waters of the North Sea.

We were pretty packed in as we left for home, but I somehow wormed my way between men and squeezed through gaps to get on deck. If it helped me *not* to get seasick then I figured I'd take the risk.

It's the ***9th April*** and we let out a cheer as we land at *Southampton* and our good old England.

As I stepped off the U.S.S. *Yale* I so wanted to kiss the ground that, as I was thinking this, a chap walked straight pass me and did just that. Now why couldn't I have just gone ahead and done it there and then, blimey, I am such a thinker and now I wish I'd been a doer.

There was even a train waiting to ride us straight out of Southampton and we were all directed to it almost immediately.

So we all gathered up our things and in the welcoming train we climbed. It didn't take us long to arrive at our destination. Really it couldn't have been more fitting, when I stop and think about it. Back at *Fovant* in Wiltshire we had come and marched right back into a familiar camp. We were informed that the following day we were allowed to return home. I think a lot of us were kind of shell shocked, it was all happening so quickly.

When we awoke very early the next morning, there seemed to be quite a commotion outside. Chaps were getting us all to hurry and get a move on because they said there was a truly great sight to be seen across from the camp. When I got to where many of the chaps were looking out towards the hills my jaw literally dropped open. "Blimey, how on earth is that possible and who made them?" Out on the sides of the hill were military badges somehow etched into the ground? As there obviously was chalk underneath the grassy hills, these badges really showed up incredibly well. They are masterpieces of the human hand. The

The SS Elephanta.

The USS Yale.

soldiers hands nonetheless, we discovered when we went along to one of the huts on the camp to ask about them.

It seemed that when one regiment, the London Rifle Brigade, started making one, it caught on and other units began to follow suit. There was even an Australian badge. Well, actually this one couldn't be missed, it was huge.

What a way to start the day and a special day at that, as we shall all soon be reunited with our families.

After tucking into some good old bread and cheese, which by the way was the best ever, and smelling the fresh air I was ready. I'd scrubbed up as best I could and given my boots a well-earned polish before setting out on the final part of my journey.

There was just one important thing to do before leaving and that was to call in at the Office and pick up my Certificate, I've been told, as I am not going to remain with Somerset Light Infantry.

I have had quite enough of "serving my country" for the while thank-you-very-much.

I started off very early as I wanted to return home on the same train as I had begun five years ago. I was heading towards Salisbury to get the train back towards Bath and then I would get on the 'slow and dirty' to Evercreech.

When I reached Queen Square Station in Bath the memories came flooding back to me. I remember how nervous I'd felt when I stood on this platform, holding my precious borrowed suitcase and a note from Mum with directions to the Headquarters. The very thought of this memory brought a smile to my face, so much so that a poor woman who was walking in my direction looked up and down herself, probably wondering if I was laughing at her. I quickly averted my glance in the opposite direction to avoid her as she walked past.

Here she comes, puffing steam and letting out large puffy clouds of white smoke. They'll turn black along our route, I thought to myself as I jumped on board. My heartbeat had quickened at the sight of her and I was truly excited. It was a mixture of all sorts of

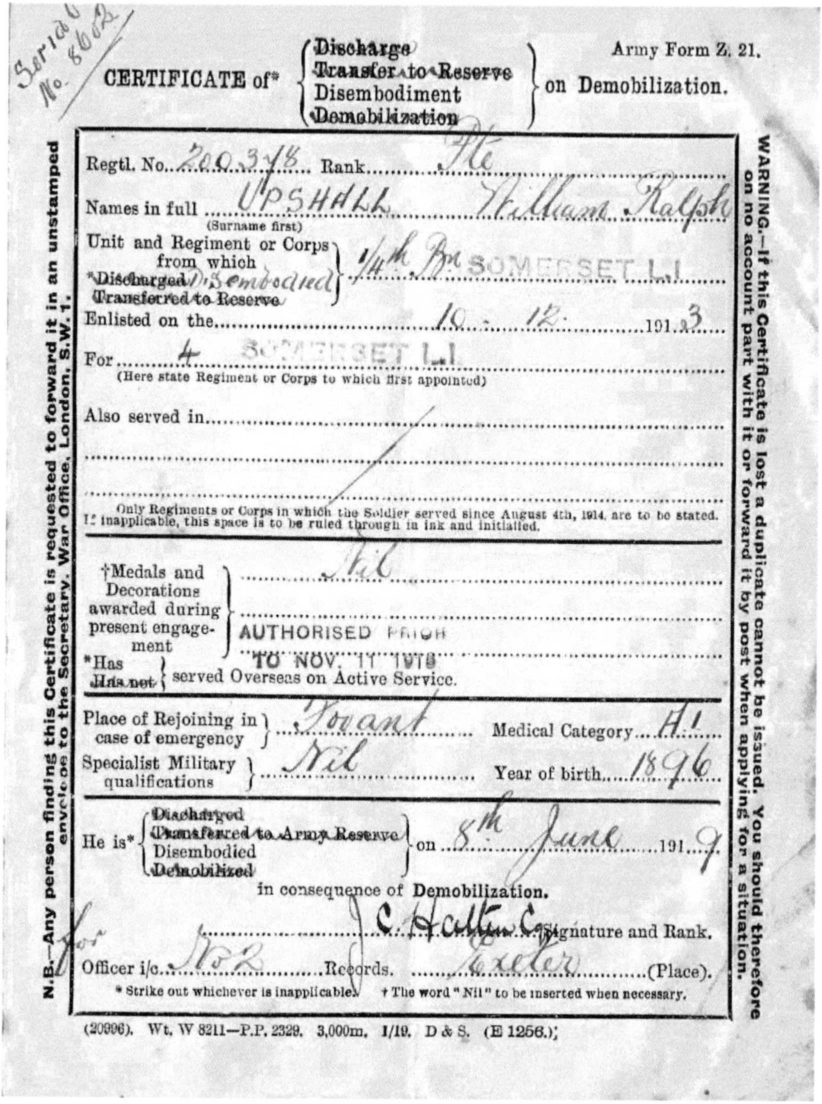

Serial No. 8602

CERTIFICATE of* {~~Discharge~~ / ~~Transfer to Reserve~~ / Disembodiment / ~~Demobilization~~} on Demobilization.

Army Form Z. 21.

Regtl. No. 200378 Rank Pte

Names in full UPSHALL William Ralph
(Surname first)

Unit and Regiment or Corps from which *~~Discharged~~ Disembodied ~~Transferred to Reserve~~ 1/4th Bn SOMERSET L.I.

Enlisted on the 10 . 12 . 1913

For 4 SOMERSET L.I.
(Here state Regiment or Corps to which first appointed)

Also served in ....

Only Regiments or Corps in which the Soldier served since August 4th, 1914, are to be stated.
If inapplicable, this space is to be ruled through in ink and initialled.

†Medals and Decorations awarded during present engagement: Nil

AUTHORISED PRIOR TO NOV. 11 1918

*Has ~~Has not~~ served Overseas on Active Service.

Place of Rejoining in case of emergency: Fovant

Medical Category: A1

Specialist Military qualifications: Nil

Year of birth: 1896

He is* {~~Discharged~~ / ~~Transferred to Army Reserve~~ / Disembodied / ~~Demobilized~~} on 8th June 1919

in consequence of Demobilization.

for C. Hatten Capt. Signature and Rank.

Officer i/c No 2 Records. Exeter (Place).

* Strike out whichever is inapplicable. † The word "Nil" to be inserted when necessary.

N.B.—Any person finding this Certificate is requested to forward it in an unstamped envelope to the Secretary, War Office, London, S.W. 1.

WARNING.—If this Certificate is lost a duplicate cannot be issued. You should therefore on no account part with it or forward it by post when applying for a situation.

(20996). Wt. W 8211—P.P. 2329. 3,000m. 1/19. D & S. (E 1256.)

"There was just one important thing to do before leaving and that was to call in at the Office and pick up my Certificate."

excitement bundled up into one huge bubble inside of me; to be sitting back on this train heading towards home, the thought of coming home and seeing Mum and Dad and my young brother, the train journey getting to Evercreech and looking out the window along the way and seeing familiar scenes and places. Oh I do hope I stay awake to enjoy every minute. I stand up to slide a window open above my head, that'll help me stay alert I think to myself.

I am by no means the only soldier on the train, but at the moment there isn't a lot of talking going on, probably we're all contemplating getting home and taking it all from there really.

I mean how do we go about changing from one minute being a soldier and just coming back from strange and terrible circumstances, to waking up tomorrow to the quiet of home life and being normal again? Blimey, I can't get my head around that one yet. Better take one day at a time I reckon and just see what happens. There is a sudden jerk of the train; the whistle lets off an enormous high-pitched noise that sends me jumping out of my seat and almost hitting the roof! I'd been so engrossed in my thoughts that I hadn't even realised we were still at the platform.

Familiar ground and my train home

THIS IS IT THEN, the last part of my journey home. As I sit and watch the English hills, fields and houses pass me by, I begin to realise how green everything looks. The fields I like in particular with their dividing hedges and odd shapes. I hadn't really noticed before, but not all the fields are square and perfect in shape, but some have almost an L-shape to them. Funny how being away from a place can make you come back and look at it in a whole new perspective. When I remember the scenery in India in particular, when I travelled by train to Wellington, I realise that parts of that journey were very stunning and almost even more so in comparison with what I am now seeing. Not that I feel bored by what I see, blimey, not at all. My heart still races when I see viaducts curving in front of the 'slow and dirty' and the tunnels we pass through still bring excitement. It's just that now I realise that another country can be just as interesting, if not more thrilling with its landscapes and hidden gems. The past five years have certainly opened up my eyes to a whole different level.

I am grateful that the English temperature is what it is. The unbearable Indian heat and that of Mesopotamia will not be missed one bit. Already I have smelt the difference in the air. I say smelt instead of felt, as the crispness I noticed when I awoke this morning at the camp, was a sheer joy. The earths smell even is a thing not to be ignored and I shall not do it ever again. I suppose I have taken most of my surroundings for granted and now come home to finally appreciate it all over again.

Oh, the carriage starts rocking and shaking from side to side and I imagine we have passed Moorewood Sidings. Looking out of the window my thoughts are correct and confirm that the poor train is struggling as it comes along the Mendip Hills of Somerset. It won't be long now. I just notice colours along the embankment and realise they are daffodils. When was the last time I saw a daffodil? Blimey, am I going mad thinking about a daffodil? I am sure I saw flowers in the places we stayed in India and anyway I remember seeing colour for pity sake. No I was more impressed with other things at the time, like their oxen and the girls and women carrying things on their heads and then there were those beautiful shells on the Andamen Islands. I wonder if Mum got hers alright and did she get them all in one piece?

I take a moment to look at my Certificate that I'd just received, before putting it in between my notebook. Oh hadn't I ever mentioned anything about my little notebook? Well, nothing really special, just some notes I jotted down for reference sometime later on maybe. You know, just in case I ever wish to explain my whereabouts during the War.

"Protection Certificate and Certificate of Identity" is what it's called. Blimey I reckon I had better take-care-not-to-loose-this little-piece-of-paper!

I must concentrate now on my whereabouts or I shall forget to step off the train. I have just realised I haven't even noticed the train stop and start each time we get to a station, that's the state of my mind right now. I must put a stop to this stupidity once and for all; I shall be a nervous wreck by the time I get off if I don't watch myself. Bill, pull yourself together.

I wonder who is at home now. As none of us knew exactly our route home and how long it would take us, nobody could write and tell anyone a date or a day. Oh well, it will be a big surprise, that's for sure.

Blimey, Evercreech New Station, hey that's my sign to leave the train. Here goes my homecoming then. I stand, pull my bag over my shoulder and stretch my knees before walking towards the door and putting my boots down onto Evercreech platform.

I stand there for a while and watch the train pull away and carry on its journey taking other soldiers and family to their destinations. I feel my stomach tighten and as I try to relax I feel a shudder. That good old saying that Mum would mention if I were nervous came into my head; 'you've got butterflies in yer stomach lad'. It brought a smile to my face and I said to myself 'yeah, that's what I've got right now'.

I was actually the only person to step out of the train here at Evercreech New Station and while I was busy collecting my thoughts and tugging at my bag over my shoulder, the only other person on the platform walked towards me. As he got a little closer I could tell he was the Station Master by his cap and he was studying his pocket watch.

"Hello there, and may I be the first to welcome you back in Evercreech. I'm assuming you be a comin' home to yer family again. Fred's the name, Frederick Courage, and who might you be?"

"Thank you Mr. Courage, I'm Bill, Bill Upshall and you'd be right in welcoming me back home to Evercreech. I've just got back from India and a long journey it's been too." I didn't know what else to say to him right there and then and Mesopotamia just seemed too long a word to get out!

"Well, I won't be a keepin' you any longer then, you carry right on there and get back to yer loved ones now."

"Can I ask what time it is please?"

"Of course you can, why it's comin up to 8 o'clock Bill".

He actually shook my hand and patted me on the back, which seemed to surprise me a bit. Without lingering any more, I did as I was told and made my way along the path and down the narrow steps onto Weston Town road.

It was still early in the morning and I wondered who would be about. I could picture Mum perhaps in the kitchen or out the back busying away. My pace quickened with these thoughts. I was sure to give her a big surprise as I walked inside the front door. Up through the back alley I marched and before I knew it there I was standing outside that door, my heart in my throat just hoping and longing for one of Mum's big hugs. I gave the door a push, as it wasn't shut, and stepped inside. My eyes had a while to focus through the little dark hall and they needed even more adjustment making my way through to the back and the kitchen. I could see Mum through the little window by the vegetable patch, carrying a basket of beetroot. I put my bag down on the floor and stepped out the back door to greet her.

I wanted to call out 'Mum' to her but I was choked and before I could eventually get it out, she'd looked up and caught sight of me.

Well, that was the surprise right there, because she just dropped her basket of beetroot, which sent it rolling back onto the garden and she just glided towards me with arms stretched wide open, calling 'Bill, oh Bill my son yer back oam safe an sound'.

There we stood holding each other tight as could be, tears running down both our cheeks with the sheer delight of seeing each other. I couldn't utter a single word, of course. I could feel all the tenseness I had in the last stages of my journey flowing literally out of my arms and through my whole body, down my legs and out through my feet! I admit it, I sobbed so hard it made my ribs hurt.

Mum pulled slightly away from me and gave me a good old look in the eyes, smiled, held my hand, led me back into the kitchen and sat me down on the nearest chair. "Let's be aving a cup a cocoa and take the weight off our feet". Mum said whilst she was already scooping some cocoa into a couple of cups and lifting the kettle off the hob and filling them with steamy water.

She poured in a measure of milk too and gave it all a good stir.

Home with Mum and I am lost for words

We must have sat looking at each other for ages. You know what I mean, when your Mum gives you that thoughtful caring once over with her eyes without uttering a single word.

I think we were still all choked up to speak actually. I certainly was. All I could do was to stretch out and hold her hand.

The warmth of the cocoa seeped into my body and I could feel it's as it passed down inside me to my stomach. It was the first time I'd had cocoa in years.

Now and then I would slip my other hand down onto my leg and pinch myself. Blimey, I'd think, am I in a dream or am I sat opposite Mum right now.

When I did eventually speak, the words came out all wrong but Mum understood me and got up to console me.

Mum showed me another newspaper cutting that she had kept which mentioned my brother Tom:

KILLED IN ACTION

PTE. TOM EDWIN UPSHALL, 7290

1st Hampshire Regiment, mentioned in despatches for conspicuous bravery in the field on November 1st, 1914, was killed in action on May 13th last. He was a son of Mr. and Mrs. Thomas Upshall, of this village and was born April 15th, 1886. He had therefore just passed the age of 29. He first joined the Hampshire Volunteers at Bournemouth, where he was at the time living, and a year later in September, 1904, enlisted into the 1st Hampshire Regiment, serving three years with the colours, one year being in Bermuda. He went there in December, 1905 and returned the following December, just in time to spend the Christmas at his own home in Evercreech. After completing at Portsmouth the remaining portion of his three years with the colours, he came back, as a reservist, to his native village, settled down and married. Very active and keen of sight, he was a good marksman, and at his last annual inspection in June 1914, did all that was required of him, not missing a single hit in shooting.

Called up when war was declared, on August 5th last, he proceeded to join his Regiment at Winchester, going thence to Colchester, and shortly after to the Front, where he remained 9 days short of 9 months, without a break. He fought through many heavy engagements, with several lucky escapes. On one occasion, a little before Christmas last, some shrapnel was found lodging in his haversack, but Upshall received no personal injury until the day he was killed. Whilst his letters home were generally cheerful, experiences related therein showed what terrible times his regiment had endured.

It continues further, mentioning the same information that Mum had sent me in one of her letters, but then it carries on:

On May 6th he wrote: - "We have been fighting now for 9 days, and just got back out of it, but I expect we shall soon be in it again. It was worse than any hell ever could be; the ground fairly shook under us, and the poisonous gases were awful. We had to put wet pads or handkerchiefs over our mouths. How I lived to get through it God only knows. For 9 days and nights we have had hardly any sleep, and not much food, and only water to drink; still we kept the Germans back, though with a big loss in our regiment. I expect you will see in the paper the list of our losses. I hope I shall never have to go through anything like it again. We are having a few days' rest, but of course we do not know a minute when we shall go in the firing line again. I hope I do not see any more of it. I think I have been through enough, nearly 9 months out here – it will be 9 months the 22nd of this month – the time soon flies. I hope the war does not last much longer. Don't trouble to send me any other papers so long as you can let me have the Shepton Journal".

On May 9th Upshall again wrote home a card, saying he was still quite well. The last communication to his relatives at home was an Expeditionary post card, written May 12th, saying – "I am quite well. Am going on well. Letter follows at first opportunity." But that promised letter has never come.

He gave his life for King and Country on the day following.

Private Tom Upshall had been married six years, and leaves a young widow with two children to mourn his loss.

Accompanying the War Office communication of the death to the widow was a communication from Lord Kitchener as follows: - "The King commands me to ensure you of the true sympathy of His Majesty and the Queen in your sorrow. – Kitchener".

When I had finished reading all of this, by which time I had gone from standing up in the kitchen to walking around the table and sitting down again, I felt so choked up that I didn't know quite what to say. My brother had gone through hell and back. What can you say after something like that?

Mum said the colour just left my face and I had started to shake.

I needed some fresh air so I walked out the back door. I was at a loss for what to do. My hands went inside my trouser pocket and I felt my packet of cigarettes. I pulled one out and lit it.

Dad was real pleased to see me back home 'in one piece', as he put it. He gave me such a hard hug when he walked in the door and saw me that it almost cracked my ribs. The strain on his face told a different story. His burden of now losing three of his eldest sons was so heavy it must have torn at his heart.

We spent that evening drinking apple cider and warming ourselves by the hearth. But do you know what, right then it was enough to be going on with.

That evening, before going up to bed, I reckoned I was going to darn right spoil myself. I fetched the old tub from the kitchen and placed it in front of the hearth that was still aglow. After boiling some water and getting the correct temperature, I had filled that tub as far as I dared go, taking in consideration me stepping into it and raising the water level, and I stripped off and eased myself down in. I'd grabbed a bar of soap too from the kitchen sink and I indulged. The sheer pleasure of soaking myself for the very first time, in this manner of course was indescribable. I have never in my life felt so relieved of a soak as I did right there and then. Blimey, I thought, I shall never complain about taking a bath ever again. Now I know what Mum used to say is very true: "you never know what you've got 'till you aven't got it".

I woke up feeling almost like a new man and I felt I could face a new day feeling more confident.

Later that morning I asked Mum about Fred and she explained that he had been in a London Hospital for several months last year and has lost an eye.

I could tell how this must have affected her and even more for poor Fred, as Mum went on to explain how this has taken its toll on him seeing as he had wished to continue his duties in the Royal Garrison as a Guard at Buckingham Palace. Obviously now he wouldn't be eligible for such a position.

Actually Mum had to sit down for a bit as it upset her so. I tried to comfort her as best I could. Blimey poor Fred is all I could think of saying to her, which wasn't helping in the slightest. Mum has always been so extremely proud of all of her sons and has often boasted to neighbours in her own way, telling them how handsome we all are. The usual comments a Mum will mention to another Mum about their offspring.

She handed me a letter that he had sent her during his time in the hospital and one part read as follows:

> "We have spent all morning lying on our stomachs behind a row of hedges watching the Germans march by. By God if anyone had coughed or sneezed we would have all been killed."

Jesse had been discharged after his prolonged sickness, which was not diagnosed and remains a mystery. Mum reckons he was very lucky because if he had gone with his regiment he most likely would have been killed as Jesse heard later that nearly all of them had died. Mum says she thinks he is looking to start up a home for his family a little nearer to here.

"I 'spec I'd best be tellin you t'other bad news meself for you ere it from someone else", Mum said looking at me in a very sad way. I started to rack my brain as who else there was and then I thought of Amy. "Is it Arthur? Has he been badly injured too?" "He'd come home anyhroad, to be with Amy and his little'uns and we all thought he were mending thur for a minute and then he died just for Christmas day. Poor Amy she were in a state and she kept saying t'woant be the same ever again Mum."

"Blimey, Mum how awful." I was beyond words by now and didn't know quite what to say. This was all too much to tackle in one day. I said I needed some air for a while and I reckon I'd take a walk up the road for a bit.

A Walk in Evercreech and a Tribute to the Soldiers Lost

I found myself walking to the village cross, where I noticed flowers had been laid on the steps there. Some of them had gone over but had still not been taken away. They didn't look odd though, in a strange way they looked as though they were lingering on in the hope of a revival of some kind.

Mum had written to me about the War Shrine that had been put here and now I stood before it, admiring it.

I sat down on the seat opposite as I felt a little light headed. I felt empty inside and strange on the outside. It had seemed out of order not to dress in my uniform this morning, in fact I probably would have worn it if Mum hadn't have already taken it away to give it 'a good old wash and scrub'. My head felt naked without a hat on and as a matter of fact I had grabbed Dad's porkpie-pie hat on the way out the front door and without even giving it another thought had popped it on my head. I'm sure he won't mind my borrowing it anyway as he doesn't wear it whilst he's working.

Its funny how habits stick with a person isn't it? About the hat I mean and needing something on my head. I didn't miss my heavy boots though, thank goodness. I remember the first time I'd started marching with them and the blisters I'd get, and anyhow they were only fit for the bin now.

Then another thought popped into my head – now what am I going to do? Besides buy myself a hat, that is.

It seemed like everyone had changed in the village and even my own family seemed different. I don't mean in a discerning way, because it's not like that, it's just we've all got older I suppose. My sister 'Queenie' has become a young lady and that is not how I remember her at all. Back then she was a teenager and different. The same goes for Cecil; he too has grown up and I hardly recognized him, although he says the same of me. He says he can't help but stare at me now and then to check I am really his brother Bill! It's so peculiar that I can't really explain it properly. On the outside we have remained similar but it is on the inside that a change has taken place and altered the way we behave. I can't seem to get my head around it to be honest with you.

I NEED TO KEEP BUSY AND FIND A JOB

I WAKE UP ONE morning with a new purpose in the day ahead of me; I need to find a job. I'd had quite enough of sitting at home and frankly it wasn't doing me any good at all. I needed to be active again and damn quick too.

Dad had said, when I mentioned it first thing this morning, they were probably still asking for men at the Milk Factory. So the Milk Factory it was then. That is where I headed for, which for me was only a small walk up to Victoria Square and just up the road on the right hand side was C & G Prideaux Limited. I walked straight through the gate and towards the Offices. I actually managed to see and speak to Mr. Charles Neale, the Manager and within twenty minutes I was back outside and heading towards home with the prospect of starting a new job the next day at the factory. I knew they were milk and cream contractors and manufactured cheese and dried milk because I'd just been told this and I felt a sigh of relief coming on. I would have a sense of order and routine back in my life and that was the best I could ask for right now.

On 19th July there were Peace Celebrations all over the place and all of us involved in the war took part in a huge procession through the village. A thanksgiving service was also held and the choirs from St. Peter's Church and the Wesleyan Chapel joined in. It was a great day and an excuse to let off steam at the end for all of us.

My brother John has been seriously ill for a while now and it could be influenza. He doesn't look too good when I go and visit him in the local hospital and I feel very worried about him.

The following week is touch and go and on 4th December 1919 we get word that he has passed away. He was 32 years old.

Dad had the following words chosen for his memorial card and I would very much like to share them with you:

Light after darkness, gain after loss,

Strength after suffering, crown after cross,
Joy after sorrow, calm after blast,
Rest after weariness, sweet rest at last.

Tom's body was never found but his name is carved on the Menin Gate along with more than 50,000 other missing men, including four men from Shepton Mallet and another man from Evercreech.

A permanent War Memorial was erected in Evercreech Cemetery the following year dedicated to those who lost their lives. It helps in so many ways and has now a purpose and is a place where anyone can go to pay their respects.

The Roll of Honour was placed on the wall inside the Parish Church where it has stayed ever since. I can only describe it as a work of art. The wooden rectangular frame is engraved with the words 'For King and Country' at the top and at the bottom with 'The Heroic Dead'. Behind the glass case lays the Roll itself with its fine embroidery depicting our country's flags and greenery including laurel leaves and the welsh thistle. Written in black ink are the words: -

'That a man lay down his life for his friends'.

Then below the Roll of Honour each initial is carefully written in Gold, with the surname in black. There are 40 souls mentioned in the Roll and Tom appears in the fifth left hand row. It catches my breath each time I look at it.

Written under the names are the words: -

'These died that we might live'

written in blue beneath: -

'To their souls whose blood was poured for their country at thy word.
Rest eternal grant O Lord'.

A brass plate below the frame says :

"This Roll of Honour was dedicated to the Glory of God and in memory of the Glorious dead as a War Shrine".

A GIRL CALLED DORIS

MUM AND DAD ARE just about coping with their latest grief, when my youngest brother Cecil drops another bombshell into their laps, explaining to us all one evening that he would also like to go to the United States. He had obviously been planning this for a while as he says he can stay with Alice and her family until he sorts himself out and he has saved up enough money to pay his own way.

He cannot be persuaded otherwise and much to the dismay of both Mum and Dad he books his passage and on the 7th April 1920 he sets sail from Southampton to New York on the S.S. Adriatic.

The air was so thick in our cottage for the next few days; you could have cut it with a knife. Dad seemed in sheer shock and you would have thought he'd lost another son. Blimey, I suppose in a way he has lost Cecil because the chances of seeing him back any time soon are neigh on impossible.

Cecil had spoken to me about wanting a change so badly and not being happy at all in Evercreech. I just had rather he'd have waited a while that's all. His argument was, of course, that there would never be a right moment to go, so it was more a question of now or never.

I shall not bore you with further details of my normal life, but I would like to explain them in short if I may. You see this very same year, 1920, does bare a great deal of importance to me as I happen upon a very charming young woman called Doris. We meet in Shepton Mallet market place. Doris looked very smart and after being introduced to her by a friend of mine, she explained that she had just been to a Wedding ceremony and that was why she was all 'dressed up'.

She was only 16 years old and I think, at first, she thought me rather too old to be interested in her as I was getting on for 23 years of age. But there was something about her and after a while we seemed to 'click'.

I didn't speak much of the war, only that I'd gone overseas to India. She said how she had helped out in her own little way by knitting lots and lots of socks for the soldiers. I could relate to this as I explained that Mum had mentioned it in one of her letters whilst I was away. Doris was only 9 years old at the time she started knitting, but she was awarded with a *medal* for knitting the most socks between 1914 and 1918! I was impressed.

Our romance blossomed and on the 20th December 1923 we got married at the Parish Church in Shepton Mallet. It was remarkably hot for the time of year and I had *'tied the knot'*.

I finally get to 'tying this knot' myself and I must admit it is the best feeling ever.

There was a moment of sadness however, when I had time to pause and look around – my dad was not here to see my glorious day. You see, Dad had passed away quite suddenly on the 30th November 1922. In that same year Cecil had married his sweetheart, Nancy, who had also emigrated from Wales and they had settled in a place called Rhode Island.

Dad had still been very unhappy the last couple of years and Mum always reckons he died of a broken heart. His grief had lingered so long after John had died. I search my thoughts and realise what Dad must have been going through. He had treasured his family and his tales of his grandfather and great grandfather came flooding back to me. He then has to 'loose' 4 of his children to this latest fashion of emigrating to a 'better life' and on top of that 2 of his sons are lost during a war.

And my photographs… well, it took me a while before actually showing them to the family. The strange thing was, no-one really thought about them until one day I sat looking at the camera and reckoned I'd better find out if they had amounted to anything. Of course, I was pleased to actually see my results and I shall keep them safe and sound, together with my diary, because who knows maybe one day I shall pass it on to my own family as a little bit of history to remember that I took part in.

"I happen upon a very charming young woman called Doris. We meet in Shepton Mallet market place."

EPILOGUE

BILL AND DORIS MOVED into Bridge Cottage, Weston Town, where his mum and dad had first lived when they came to Evercreech and he felt the better for it as, in his own mind, he was keeping his family memories close to hand. Also his mother lived in the house next door and in some way he felt he could keep 'an eye' on her so to speak.

Bill's mum passed away on 24th August 1939 at the age of 84.

Bill and Doris had a modest 4 children who they named accordingly: Ivy Lilian Doris was their first born, on 3rd March 1925 followed by my dad Eric William born on 24th October 1927, then Beryl Olive Maud born on 28th May 1930 and finally, last but not least Valerie Joy was born 14th February 1937.

Bill worked at the Milk Factory for 45 years. He was very much involved with village life and played football for Evercreech Rovers and he and Doris were also caretakers for the village hall for 25 years.

He joined the 4th Somerset (Frome) Battalion, Home Guard during WW2 and Doris worked for the Civil Defence in Evercreech.

Would you believe that 5 decades later his own son, Eric William, came upon the very same Doctor Bishop as Bill had seen in Wellington, India? He himself had just returned from the Second World War and was in the neighbouring town of Shepton Mallet. When the doctor in question heard his name he remarked that he knew his father during WW1 and had stayed with him throughout his illness. Eric was so surprised and couldn't wait to get home and tell his father that this Doctor Bishop had remembered him.

Bill was a very keen gardener and entered many of his vegetables in the local Evercreech Agricultural Show, winning many cups in the process.

He was devoted to Doris and his children, passed on stories of his family to his children and has always stayed in contact with his family in America and even had a family reunion in 1957, travelling there himself with his wife Doris.

Bill was also a very clever man and could just about put his mind to anything and everything, even down to repairing his own shoes and those of his children's.

He continued his love of life and enjoyed dressing up for just about anything to have a laugh. He would even take part on Carnival floats.

He never left the house without a trilby hat and later in his life this changed to a tweed country flat cap or similar for the summer months.

He didn't talk very much about his time in India and Mesopotamia. In fact his youngest daughter recalls that if the latter country was ever mentioned, his children thought he'd made it up! Of India he would only talk of such tales of the dhobis who washed his clothes and he would mention the big mother-of-pearl shell that he had brought back.

At 86 years of age Bill celebrated his Diamond Wedding Anniversary with Doris still looking as good and lively as ever.

He treasured just about everything he had and his precious shell that he had bought on the Andaman Islands for his mum, had been passed on to him and Doris, who gave it pride of place in their own home.

Bill died on the 23rd June 1987 at Shepton Mallet District Hospital. He was 90 years of age.

I guess you could say that his character, skills and thoughtfulness have also been passed on to his own children and they, in turn, have passed on these skills to his total of 10 grandchildren.

Before I even started to put pen to paper, I decided to drive to the nearest town, Shepton Mallet, and pay a visit to the local library. In the War section I looked at books relating to WW1 and came across a book called "Answering the Call" by John F. Mackie. It caught my eye because it mentioned the exact same battalion as my grandfather was in. I decided to borrow this book and take it home to read.

After being inspired by the book, my next step was to sort out the dates and places listed in Bill's diary. I felt I shouldn't even be handling this diary too much just in case I did damage the pages or worsen the already fading handwriting. I re-typed the pages and printed them out and carefully slid the book back into its leather wallet for safe keeping. I was equally worried about the photographs, so I scanned each one and saved them on my laptop. Thank goodness for technology. Luckily on the reverse of each photograph Bill had written the name of the place in pencil and this was also still readable. My next step was to do some research.

When I returned the library book I walked up the High Street of Shepton Mallet and walked into the Information Centre at the top of the street. I had no idea how I would be able to discover where Bill had enlisted or where to go with all this information. A very kind lady made me aware of the Somerset Heritage Centre and that I could most probably find answers to most of my questions there. The Centre was in Taunton and with the help of Google I soon found the website and directions on how to find it and it also listed many research guides.

Dad insisted on coming with me even when I explained that it might take many hours and involve looking through old dusty books. I was really worried if he would be up to the journey but, of course, I couldn't exactly say that now could I? I realised that he wanted to be part of the book too in any way that he could, even if it only meant holding each page as I looked!

So, armed with a notebook, the typed pages of Bill's diary and my reading glasses we left early on a Monday morning towards Taunton.

As Bill had carefully written exactly which part of the Somerset Light Infantry he was in and where he had been sent to, I already had a head start.

That day was to be the beginning of many more trips to the Centre. I cannot explain the excitement that both myself and my dad experienced after discovering the exact documents to verify all the dates and the places in Bill's diary. It was tiring, I admit to that and quite demanding at times. I was so proud of Dad though, because he was there with me to hold the pages and help read them, as many were also handwritten accounts from Commanding Officers in charge of the Battalion. He was patient and never complained, although I did notice the huge sigh of relief the minute I 'called it a day', after looking at my watch and realising 'the day' was now the evening.

One day we had to go to Taunton Hospital as appointments had been arranged for some scans and that's when reality finally struck.

On the journey back home in the car, Dad suddenly says "I'm a gonner". I looked across at him and I could see tears running down his cheeks. I held his hand for most of the trip back, roads permitting of course. I could see Mum on the back seat clutching her seat belt and staring out of the window. Nothing else was said. I had no radio on; there was no chattering away like we would normally have done. There was just the silence. It was our worst journey ever. I felt like pulling over the minute the opportunity came, to give Dad a big hug, but I knew he wanted to get home as soon as possible.

When I woke up the next morning, I led in my bed thinking about Dad and how I should attempt this writing. Then it suddenly plopped into my head. I must 'be' Bill. I must try and feel 'his' thoughts and make the journey with him as opposed to making it for him. I knew from the very beginning that this would be nearly impossible to do, but I was willing to give it a try. You see I wanted to create a 'story' rather than tell a 'report' with places and dates.

You should have seen the look on Dad's face when he caught me one afternoon sitting behind my laptop ticking away, he was grinning from ear to ear.

On New Year's Eve Dad took a turn for the worse and luckily I had my oldest sister Carolyn and her husband Patrick with me, because we hardly managed to lift him into the stair lift and up to his bed, he was so weak. I shall never forget those last few weeks of my father's life. He knew how bad he was and I remember him saying "I won't be going downstairs anymore, will I". What do you answer to that? All we could do was to be there for him, day and night and that's what we did. We had it all worked out you see. I would sleep with Mum in one bedroom whilst Carolyn and Trisha would 'camp out' on the floor close to Dad's bed and then we'd swop and I would 'camp out'.

The support from Dorothy House and the District nurses was unbelievable. Also one of the local G.P's was particularly kind and caring to Dad, Dr. Geoff Sharp.

Our dad passed away on 13th January 2012 at home, comfortably tucked in bed, with his 'girls' at his side.

I had vowed to finish his father's book on his behalf (giving my promise to finish it one day at his bedside) and was only too sorry that he wasn't going to be able to read it. However I had, luckily enough, printed out the first part of my story for him to read, as I could tell how curious he would get and wonder how I was doing. He had read it, smiled at me, laughed a little and had given his approval.

When I felt strong in mind to pick up where I had left off, I came against other barriers. I couldn't leave Mum on her own too long and even when I would sit behind my laptop, after an hour Mum would call out "are you still on that blessed computer, because it's time you stopped and give your eyes some rest". Bless her, she didn't like it one bit. I would try to do as much as I could whilst Mum had her afternoon nap. I even made an attempt to sit in the same room as Mum, just to keep her company so she would know where I was, but it didn't really work out. I felt I couldn't concentrate, or I'd happen to look up and catch sight of Mum looking at me, then she would mutter to herself, go 'tut, tut' and smile at me.

A year went by and we were managing quite well, although I knew deep down that Mum was grieving for Dad. They had, after all, been together since 1949 when they got married and actually even before then, as they had known each other at the age of 16. It's a lifetime of companionship which is suddenly severed away. I can't begin to comprehend how that must be; having not made it past 17 years of marriage myself I'm sorry to admit.

Mum passed away on 12th September 2014 after heart failure. She knew she was dying as all she could manage to say whilst in Yeovil Hospital was "get me out of here and back home". So that's what we did. Me, Carolyn and my youngest sister Trisha; we asked for arrangements to be made to get her back home as soon as possible. Yeovil District Hospital staff did wonders to put this in motion and arranged all the necessary equipment we would need to care for our mum at home.

It was just horrendous to have to go through almost the same as we had done with Dad. We did it though, exactly as with our dad, taking it in turns to sit with her during the night, having support from Bluebird carers and the local nurses. Actually most of the District Nurses remembered us as they had cared for Dad too. One afternoon as I was sitting at Mum's bedside she suddenly said "if this is dying then I don't think much of it". It's just typical of Mum to say that. I didn't give a reply but I held her hand. All three of us did just that as she took her last breath.

I am telling you this because it's what has kept me going ever since. Like the cogs on a wheel. If they fall away the wheel will stop turning. My "cogs" felt like they had crumbled around me, but I have been determined to hang on to the one promise I had made to Dad and writing this has helped to keep me strong and has given me a new purpose in my life and keep the memory of my family alive. Plus the fact that I am now house sitting whilst the unfortunate sale of our family home awaits its new owners.

I would like to mention a very poignant occurrence, if I may, whilst Dad was ill, that my own son Marcel and his wife Kimberley were expecting their firstborn child. Dad knew this while he lay in his bed and would often ask me if their baby had been born yet. My answer was always "no Dad, not yet". It was almost as if Dad was trying to delay the inevitable until the baby was born.

Dad died just a day before my son's wife gave birth to a baby boy, who they called Jason. It is the strangest of feelings to be grieving the loss of your father and a moment later wanting to rejoice at the news of becoming a grandmother.

Well, I have become once again a grandmother since writing this, to another grandson, born this time into my daughter Natascha's arms and her partner Raymond. Little Deejay was born one month before my Mum started to take a turn for the worse.

Whether I have been successful in my writing can only be anticipated in the reactions of those who actually pick up my story and read it. Maybe I have asked too much of myself. I can only say this: through writing about Bill I have opened my own eyes and journeyed back in time. I have met my ancestors for the first time and actually looked into their eyes. I've followed their footsteps and even met and written to relatives I hadn't seen before. I have studied war stories and maps of India and the then Mesopotamia which I hadn't done before.

I have been so engrossed in the past for the last couple of years that instead of coming back to this century I have found myself writing 1915 on various cheques and correspondence instead of 2015! My laptop has been 'red hot' as Mum would definitely have said, as she said this when I'd only been on it a few hours. What would she think now when it's on all day!

There are certain parts of my story that I can but only begin to scrape the mere surface of what possibly did happen. True fear can only be experienced by the beholder.

Thank you Dad for giving me the honour of writing about your father and thank you for helping me re-unite with my ancestors in a way in which I probably would never have done.

Thank you for this project Dad, which has been undoubtedly my solace in grieving for both you and Mum. It most certainly has helped in my healing process and has kept me busy throughout the duration the house (our home) has been up 'for sale'. (Yet another unfortunate decision which has had to be made). My drive to finish this story has kept me going and 5 years and 2 grandchildren later I am reaching the final hurdle.

My Mum and Dad – Eric and Marjorie Upshall.

REFERENCES

The Somerset Heritage Centre, Brunel Way, Langford Mead, Norton Fitzwarren, Taunton, Somerset.

The Light Bob Gazette, 4th Battalion Somerset Light Infantry, 1914-1919

Kelly's Directory of Somerset, 1910-1919

Wikipedia

Google Maps

Shepton Mallet Public Library

Forces War Records

Light Infantry Office, Somerset

Ancestry.co.uk

The National Archives

The History of Somerset Yeomanry

Fovant Badges.com

Excerpts and Extracts: An American Officer fights in Iraq with the British in WW1.

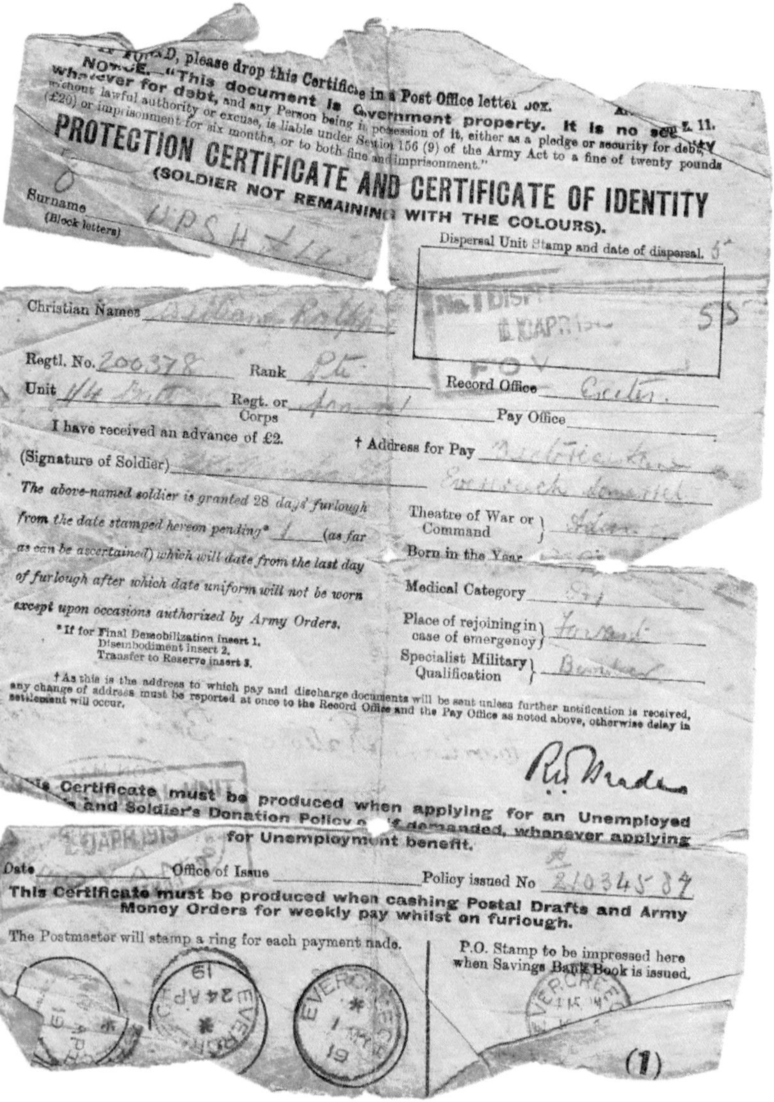

...D, please drop this Certificate in a Post Office letter box.

NOTICE.—"This document is Government property. It is no security whatever for debt, and any Person being in possession of it, either as a pledge or security for debt, without lawful authority or excuse, is liable under Section 156 (9) of the Army Act to a fine of twenty pounds (£20) or imprisonment for six months, or to both fine and imprisonment."

PROTECTION CERTIFICATE AND CERTIFICATE OF IDENTITY

(SOLDIER NOT REMAINING WITH THE COLOURS).

Surname (Block letters) UPSHALL

Dispersal Unit Stamp and date of dispersal.

Christian Names William Ralph

Regtl. No. 200378 Rank Pte

Unit 1/4 Batt. Regt. or Corps

Record Office Exeter.

Pay Office

I have received an advance of £2.

(Signature of Soldier)

† Address for Pay

The above-named soldier is granted 28 days' furlough from the date stamped hereon pending 1 (as far as can be ascertained) which will date from the last day of furlough after which date uniform will not be worn except upon occasions authorized by Army Orders.*

* If for Final Demobilization insert 1.
Disembodiment insert 2.
Transfer to Reserve insert 3.

Theatre of War or Command

Born in the Year

Medical Category

Place of rejoining in case of emergency

Specialist Military Qualification

† As this is the address to which pay and discharge documents will be sent unless further notification is received, any change of address must be reported at once to the Record Office and the Pay Office as noted above, otherwise delay in settlement will occur.

...is Certificate must be produced when applying for an Unemployed ...n and Soldier's Donation Policy ... if demanded, whenever applying for Unemployment benefit.

Date Office of Issue Policy issued No 210345 84

This Certificate must be produced when cashing Postal Drafts and Army Money Orders for weekly pay whilst on furlough.

The Postmaster will stamp a ring for each payment made.

P.O. Stamp to be impressed here when Savings Bank Book is issued.

(1)

Bill's Protection Certificate and Certificate of Identity which he carried with him throughout the War.

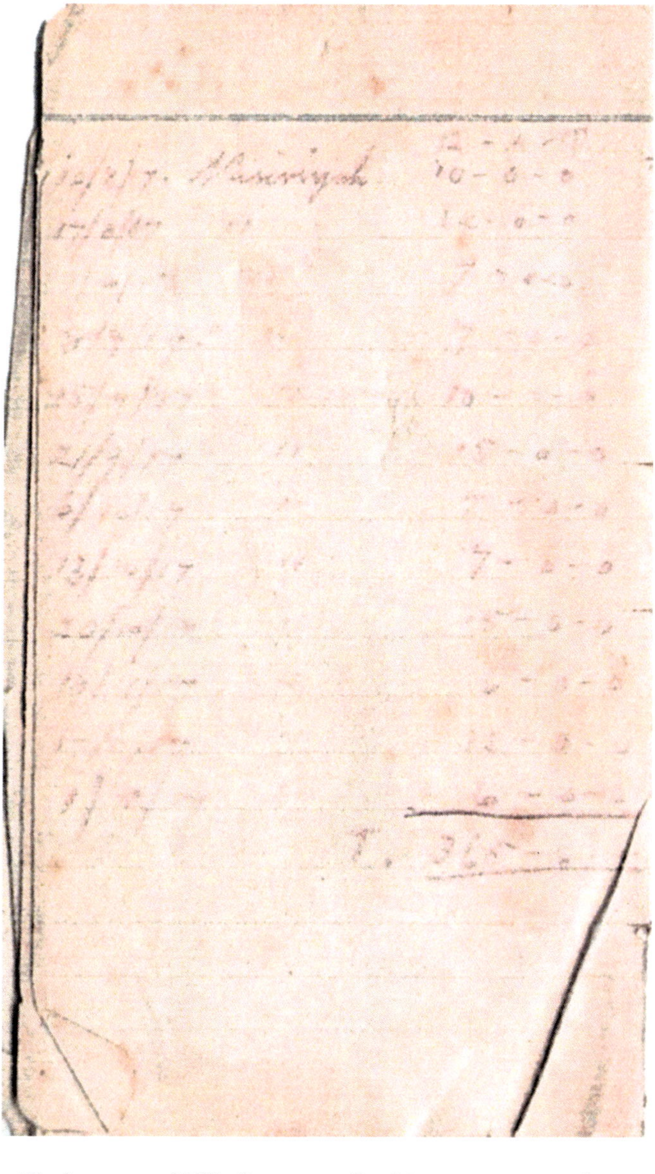

The last page of Bill's diary, recording his pay on various dates.

About the Author

Jeanette Upshall was born in 21 Bowns Close, Evercreech, Near Shepton Mallet, Somerset in 1958 and moved, at the age of 5 years old, with her parents and older sister to "Mildura", Weymouth Road, Evercreech. She met a Dutchman in Germany during a holiday, couldn't get him out of her mind and in 1982 they were married in St. Peter's Church, Evercreech and she moved to Lelystad, Holland. She has two married children, a boy and a girl, and two grandsons. She later moved to Almere, Holland and after a divorce decided to move back to Evercreech, where she has cared for her mother and father.

❖ ❖ ❖